Poverty in the United States

Poverty in the United States

Developing Social Welfare Policy for the Twenty-First Century

Andrew W. Dobelstein

palgrave
macmillan

First published in 2014 by
PALGRAVE MACMILLAN®
in the United States—a division of St. Martin's Press LLC,
175 Fifth Avenue, New York, NY 10010.

Where this book is distributed in the UK, Europe and the rest of the world,
this is by Palgrave Macmillan, a division of Macmillan Publishers Limited,
registered in England, company number 785998, of Houndmills,
Basingstoke, Hampshire RG21 6XS.

Palgrave Macmillan is the global academic imprint of the above companies
and has companies and representatives throughout the world.

Palgrave® and Macmillan® are registered trademarks in the United States,
the United Kingdom, Europe and other countries.

ISBN: 978–1–137–48547–2

Library of Congress Cataloging-in-Publication Data

Dobelstein, Andrew W.
    Poverty in the United States : developing social welfare policy for the
21st century / by Andrew W. Dobelstein.
        pages cm
    Includes bibliographical references and index.
    ISBN 978–1–137–48547–2 (alk. paper)
        1. Public welfare—United States. 2. Poverty—United States.
    3. Social service—United States. 4. United States—Social policy.
    5. Poverty—United States. I. Title.

HV95.D615 2014
362.5'5610973—dc23   2014026293

A catalogue record of the book is available from the British Library.

Design by Newgen Knowledge Works (P) Ltd., Chennai, India.

First edition: December 2014

10 9 8 7 6 5 4 3 2 1

Contents ✑

Illustrations ∽

TABLES

BOXES

FIGURES

Preface ◆

In 1958, the Russell Sage Foundation published a book by Harold Wilensky and Charles Lebeaux titled *Industrial Society and Social Welfare*. As the name implies, Wilensky and Lebeaux sought to link the development of American capitalism with an emerging need for an expanded social welfare system. Among their many observations, they stated, in part,

> The older doctrines of individualism, private property and free market, and of minimum government provided a clear-cut definition of welfare as "charity for unfortunates." The newer values of social democracy—security, equality, humanitarianism—undermine the notion of "unfortunate classes" in society. All people are regarded as having needs, which ipso facto become a legitimate claim on the whole society.[1]

This was a highly controversial statement at the time, and it probably remains even more provocative today. Our country has gone through the second largest economic calamity in modern American history, and in spite of the personal economic hardships inflicted by the Great Recession, the "newer values" of which they wrote have yet to take hold. Social welfare remains trapped in the "older doctrines," and as a result American social welfare has failed to reduce poverty in the long run or to cushion personal economic agony in the present.

I began my research, teaching, and providing assistance to people in poverty and the organizations that struggle to help them, with the conviction that the incremental social welfare advances I observed and studied would move to the point where the recognition of individual economic needs would, indeed, become legitimate claims on the whole of the American enterprise. It seemed that the "older doctrines" were being left behind, and this was the message I was bringing to my students. But over the years, it became clearer and clearer that such an American commitment remained well outside our grasp. Yes, there were new programs that provided resources for poor people. Yes, there were additions to and expansions of Social Security that broadened out its original mission. And even while some of the social welfare programs changed in punitive ways, it still seemed like American social welfare policy was headed toward a comprehensive safeguard against the unpredictable economic vagaries demonstrated so severely at various stages in our history.

But as American poverty remain fixed in spite of the new programs, I began to conclude that the very foundation of our social welfare programs was simply too weak to carry the weight of increasing social welfare demands brought about by America's social and economic changes. These conclusions were affirmed by the Great Recession and the failure of our present social welfare system to do what the creators of the Social Security Act expected it to do: provide a cushion for individuals caught in the vortex of economic events.

America's older doctrines, which accepted "charity for unfortunates," drew a bold line between those who were unfortunate and those who were simply irresponsible, and the new values sidestepped the issue. I dodge these debates, too, simply because they cannot be resolved through public policy. In the same way that rain falls on everyone, both the just and the unjust, social welfare policy concerns the whole, not the individual parts. Social welfare policy speaks to the condition of poverty, not to the individual characteristics of poor people. From this personal perspective, I am well aware of many groups of Americans who live their lives directed by traditional Puritan ethics, and they believe that everyone would be better off if others did so, too. I am also well aware of many small towns and communities scattered across America that frame community life by such values. In one of my favorite small towns in rural America, the Presbyterian church plays Christian hymns at noon each day from speakers atop its stately spire, and no business is conducted before noon on Sundays. These are important values that guide individuals in their everyday activities, but they are not a foundation capable of the development of social welfare policy.

Those who would prefer to discuss poverty as personal problems rather than structural economic ones may also be uncomfortable about my preference for cash as a way to reduce poverty rather than insisting that changing individuals, or changing social structures most effectively eases poverty. Concentrating on what I call "cash support social welfare" does not disavow other dimensions of poverty. Instead this more concise approach recognizes that our social welfare system already provides considerable amounts of cash directly to the poor, that poverty continues to be measured monetarily, and that building a better foundation under our existing cash distribution social welfare system offers a less idealized, but more pragmatic, effort to reduce poverty than other alternatives, including simply continuing to tinker with existing social welfare programs.

America has tumbled into the twenty-first century dragging its twentieth-century social, economic, and political baggage along with it. The election of Barak Obama as president was met with the enthusiasm of new beginnings after the period when America had lost respect abroad and confidence in government at home. But the new national leadership had to unbundle the leftover problems first—an unfinished, unpaid for war and the most serious economic event since the Great Depression of 1929–34, as well as the long-standing problems of racial and sexual discrimination. The resulting national political intransigence has suppressed this early optimism, leaving our nation struggling to regain its former luster. Urging a reduction in poverty, and proposing a new foundation for our social welfare system appear particularly unsuitable in today's political climate. Yet the periods of uncertainty and reticence often give voice to new ideas. America will break out of her present malaise, and when she does, she will need the energy of fresh designs.

I am indebted to many people who have helped me move beyond my traditional views of social welfare well enough to write this book. My students over the past years consistently assaulted my traditional views to the point that I had to think seriously about what has gone wrong with America's social welfare enterprise. More recently, several colleagues and critics disputed my comments and sharpened my conclusions. I benefited from conversations with Max Skidmore before I began this project, and Albert Field, Ivan Lakos, and Karl Bauman who commented on parts of the manuscript. I also benefited from the wise council of Erskin Bowles. Most of all I am fortunate to have a caring wife, Carol Candler, who often waited patiently for me to lift my head from the computer so we could talk. Of course I bear full responsibility for the materials that follow, not them.

William C. Friday served as the leader of the University of North Carolina system from 1956 to 1986, and died on October 12, 2012, the university's 219th birthday. His iconic stature is best understood by his concern for others, particularly the poor. In my few encounters with him, he urged me to continue my efforts to reduce poverty, and he firmly believed in a social welfare system that reflected the "newer values." It is therefore fitting that this book be dedicated to Bill Friday, not in his memory, but to the legacy he left the rest of us, to enshrine social welfare as the jewel in America's crown.

ANDREW DOBELSTEIN
Chapel Hill, North Carolina
October 2014

Introduction ❧

*T*he *Webster's New Collegiate Dictionary* defines shame as "a painful emotion caused by...impropriety: a condition of humiliating disgrace or disrepute: something that brings strong regret, censure or reproach."[1] Being poor in America is improper; it is humiliating and disgraceful, not only for the poor but also for all Americans who tolerate it. The poor are criticized as if they have failed, but it is our nation that has fallen short of its commitments. Poverty in America is ignominy. The wealthiest nation in the world tolerates over 15 percent of its residents living in poverty, including more than 20 percent of its children! Poverty is not only agony for those who are poor, but it is humiliating for America, who prides herself on an economic system that has raised the standard of living beyond any other. If America is not ashamed of our persistent poverty, it should be.

Americans protect themselves from the shame of poverty by reciting cherished American beliefs in individualism, self-sufficiency, and personally responsible behavior. True, many poor make bad choices. True, many prefer not to work. True, many have low expectations, poor self-esteem, and objectionable social graces. Whether these personal characteristics are the causes of poverty or the consequences of poverty is debatable, but there can be no debate that those who are poor and those who are not poor share these personal characteristics. These traits interact with America's political and economic systems that lead some into poverty, most into ordinariness, and a few into exceptional wealth and power. Many Americans, poor and non-poor alike, have fallen short of their obligations as citizens, but America has failed to live up to her commitments to her citizens as well. Poverty is an individual experience of interaction with the whole of American society. While individuals are held accountable for their personal economic well-being, the nation holds responsibility for the economic conditions that propel some to economic success and others to poverty.

America always has held polarizing views about her responsibility toward the poor. The urban poverty that grew out of the Industrial Revolution was met with feeble charitable initiatives originating in America's churches, and soon this charity work became structured through the creation of Charity Organization Societies. A strictly private endeavor with backing from religious organizations, Charity Organization Societies became America's foundation for helping the poor. Based on a system of individualizing and treating the poor through a scientific method, these societies sought to determine the unique characteristics that caused an individual to become poor; combined with friendly advice, encouragement, and "right moral persuasion," the poor person could be "rehabilitated" and, more importantly, public funds to support the family or individual were not necessary. This approach to poverty fit only too well with the evolving ideology of Social Darwinism, a social construction created by Herbert Spencer (1820–1903) from the work of Charles Darwin (1809–82) and advanced by sociologist William Graham Sumner (1840–1910). Summer's laissez-faire conclusions about government intervention into the lives of the poor were adopted by the philanthropists of the day, such as Andrew Carnegie, and social treatment of the poor by Scientific Charity became the foundation for modern social work.

There are times, however, when Americans have been forced to view their economic and political structures as causes of poverty. Certainly the Great Depression (circa 1929–35) confronted Americans with structural poverty. One-third of America's labor force was unemployed. Charities were overwhelmed. Francis Townsend raised the voice of older people in poverty when he advocated for an old-age pension for the aged who were unable to work.[2] The political consequences of that economic calamity called for a change from America's reluctance to use public resources to support the growing numbers of poor, and Congress responded with America's Social Security Act, acknowledging that our government must and can create a new social welfare structure when it is called for. Michael Harrington's galvanizing polemic, *The Other America*, stimulated public awareness of poverty, and out of this consciousness-raising, President Lyndon Johnson created a "War on Poverty," and Congress gave America the Economic Opportunity Act in 1964 and Medicare and Medicaid in 1965. Yet for all these social welfare enlargements, and not inconsequently, all the money spent on them, poverty in America has not dropped below double digits for the past 50 years. The social programs America's poor enjoy today remain in little more than a social welfare holding pattern, rather than being a social welfare safety net.

The present moment in American history provides another opportunity for our nation to face endemic poverty. The Great Recession (circa

2009–12) reminded us that poverty exists and that economic disasters concentrate at the bottom of the economic ladder, increasing the amount of poverty and making poverty more intolerable for those who have experienced it for years. Our Great Recession has exposed gaping holes in the social programs so laboriously crafted over the past 75 years. They simply failed to protect against economic calamity for millions of Americans caught in an economic vortex created from this manmade world of ours. Individual bad choices alone did not drive people into the Great Recession's poverty. America's economic structure collapsed and dragged many into its quagmire. If security determines the projection of America's political economy, then the Great Recession provides an opportunity to examine the personal insecurity of poverty in the fresh light of twenty-first-century economic and political failures it exposed.

It seems ironic that as the Great Recession winds down, the economic distance between America's richest and poorest has grown wider than at any time during the past 100 years. At the same time, when America's social programs are needed most, the Great Recession has ushered in a wave of political conservatism challenging the efficacy of America's social welfare undertakings, pushing politicians to reduce social welfare spending. Whether sequestration can reduce the national debt may be debatable, but there is no debate that it will increase the hardship of poverty. Present social welfare efforts simply failed to protect people from slipping into poverty, nor have these programs been successful in reducing the amount of poverty America continues to endure. The social welfare fallout from the Great Recession pleads for needed review of our social welfare commitments.

Although the Great Recession of 2009–12 has abated, its ruins are scattered about the country in lost homes, lost jobs, long-term unemployment, and families scrambling to regain their former economic foothold. The federal government has been able to save the banking industry and General Motors, albeit with fewer jobs and Detroit in bankruptcy. By all economic measures, however, the economy is mending, but the welfare of America's people is much less positive. The sharp peak in poverty during the Great Recession gradually has been settling back to its pre-recession levels, but the economic losses individuals suffered during this time may be slow to come back, if they ever do. Poverty remains a fixture in twenty-first-century America. Generous public spending has supported various business enterprises in the hope of nurturing an economic recovery, with an idealistic vision that an improved economy will, at long last, lift Americans out of poverty. America's confrontation with poverty over the years shows the fallacy of this belief. Retooling the economic system without retooling the social welfare system will only lead to more inequality, preserve the heritage of poverty, and avoid the obligatory economic security sought for twenty-first-century Americans.

AMERICA'S IMAGINARY "SAFETY NET"

The Great Recession was a failure of America's economic structure, accompanied by a failed social welfare instrument. The experiences from Great Recession should dispel any idea of an American social safety net. The myriad of social welfare programs, mostly anchored in the Social Security Act of 1935, that provide a loosely connected variety of poor people with cash, social, and medical services, fell far short of catching them as they tumbled off the economic ladder. There are over two thousand such programs funded by federal and state tax dollars and provided to eligible people, not all of them in poverty.[3] During the recession this disjointed, twisted assortment of services and cash payments were difficult to access, skimpy in their provisions, and attached to the economic elements that caused individuals such distress in the first place. These social initiatives have no uniform eligibility procedures, and no common objective. Different programs have different rules. Provision of benefits revealed their inadequacy once people obtained eligibility. Unemployment payments, for example, were less than poverty levels in most of the states and became exhausted for some of the most vulnerable unemployed. Most significant of all, the resources that were available usually depended on some form of employment; for example there are no Earned Income Tax Credits if people are not working. Unemployment benefits are temporary, forcing people to find vanishing jobs, and loss of employment means loss of time and income necessary to accumulate Social Security benefits in later years.

CONCENTRATION ON FORMS OF CASH SUPPORT

Chapter 1 reviews America's major efforts to reduce poverty through a prolonged, haphazard combination of social service programs and programs that provide poor people with cash. While both may be important, this book focuses on the cash support initiatives of America's social welfare architecture as the most effective way to reduce poverty. America distributes a large amount of cash directly to the poor and non-poor— over $895.9 billion under the authority of the Social Security Act alone and another $138 billion in related cash support through the Earned Income Tax Credit (EITC) and the Supplemental Nutrition Assistance Program (SNAP, formerly the Food Stamp Program) (see Appendix I.1). Modernizing existing cash support programs by focusing them more acutely on people in poverty, particularly on those program shortcomings exposed during the Great Recession, will improve America's social welfare infrastructure and have a profound effect on reducing poverty.

Two of the most comprehensive kinds of cash support programs—which are particularly sensitive to the needs of people in poverty—are found under the authority of the Social Security Act: social insurance programs, which include the Social Security Retirement Program and the Disability Insurance Program, most often referred to together as Social Security, and a program that provides cash to unemployed workers, the Unemployment Insurance Program. The development of these two social insurance programs is discussed in Chapter 3, shedding light on how they became more contestable as their specific programs changed, but their basic structures remained anchored by early twentieth-century economic and political assumptions.

The Social Security Act also contains two forms of cash *financial assistance* for people without sufficient income, which are made up of financial assistance for the aged and disabled (Supplemental Security Income, SSI) and financial assistance for Dependent Children, recreated as Temporary Assistance to Needy Families (TANF) in 1996. The development of these programs is discussed in Chapter 4; they, too, have become less and less effective at addressing poverty over the years. Thus, there are four basic programs under the authority of the Social Security Act that provide direct cash support to people eligible to receive it and comprises the major share of cash assistance.

The EITC is the fifth of the nation's cash assistance programs. It was first created in 1975 as a way to encourage labor force participation by supplementing low wages with a federal tax credit for workers who had children. It has been expanded at least five major times by enlarging the beneficiary base and increasing benefit levels, but without changes to its fundamental income tax policy assumptions. EITC not only works as a tax credit for low- and medium-income working individuals and couples, but it distributes cash as well when the tax credit exceeds the amount of taxes owed. Thus EITC is a *refundable* tax credit, a unique modification of the generally understood role of tax credits. In 1979, EITC was combined with the Child Tax Credit. Even though it is a credit against the taxes a worker owes, the Internal Revenue Service and the Congressional Budget Office consider EITC a cash transfer program, and thus it is included as part of this cash support discussion.

Supplemental Nutrition Assistance Program (SNAP) is a sixth significant program of cash assistance. SNAP is the successor to the Food Stamp program administered by the US Department of Agriculture. Like EITC, SNAP does not find its reason for being as a program to provide cash directly to individuals; rather, SNAP provides a substitute for cash with an electronic card that is used like a debit card in food stores for certain kinds of food. It is an important income maintenance program for people in or nearly in poverty that enables them to purchase food directly. For most discussions, SNAP is considered a cash transfer program although eligible people do not actually receive cash. The erosion of the ability of both EITC and SNAP to reduce poverty is discussed in Chapter 5.

The programs that make up America's cash support commitments, therefore, fall into three interlaced classes: social insurance, financial assistance, often called welfare, and cash subsidies in the form of tax credits (EITC) and food support (SNAP). All three classes of these cash support programs also share a common dynamic: work plays an important role in their benefit structures. The social insurances are used for those who have worked. The social assistance programs are earmarked for those who cannot work. Tax credits and SNAP are financial resources provided to those who are working. Each of these programs commands a primary poverty-reducing capacity through direct and indirect infusion of cash into the economic budgets of the poor. These six programs also possess existing legislative authority, but their administrative mandates lack a consistency necessary for effective engagement with poverty. They do not constitute a social welfare umbrella; instead they provide cash support to the poor and low-income people as a social welfare by-product. These cash support programs taken together have the financial capacity to buoy up individual financial resources quickly, lessen long-term economic suffering, and significantly reduce poverty, but they require refashioning to meet twenty-first-century expectations. Chapter 6 proposes how all six programs must be modernized with a foundation appropriate to the social welfare needs of twenty-first-century Americans that will reduce poverty.

THE OUTDATED SOCIAL WELFARE FOUNDATION

Most of the debate about lessons learned during this recession focused on political proposals to protect the American economy from a similar fate in the future. Little attention, however, has been given to any lessons that might have been learned about America's commitment to protect individuals from the fate they suffered during this economically destabilizing time. The social welfare structures that were created in 1935, repaired in the early 1970s, and modified almost yearly until the present time, proved inadequate, because like the banking laws that failed to prevent the recession, the cash support programs failed to protect Americans from slipping into poverty. The economy relied on nineteenth-century suppositions that no longer had validity in twenty-first-century America. Conventions underlying the obligation to provide economic security for Americans are also based on nineteenth-century beliefs, and they proved just as inadequate to protect individuals as those failed economic assumptions that fueled the Great Recession.

Fundamentally, closely tethered to work cash support evaporates when there are no jobs. Social Security, the very backbone of the cash safety net was unable to protect retired workers and their families from personal economic losses during the Great Recession, and Unemployment Insurance, with its byzantine assortment of state rules and regulations provided extremely limited protection to those who lost jobs. Job loss reduced the benefits of the EITC, forcing an expanded use of Supplemental Nutrition Program, without nearly enough resources to meet the demands placed on it. Other forms of cash financial assistance, such as TANF, were reduced as jobs were lost and state and national revenues dwindled, forcing austerity measures on the economically afflicted. While the Social Security Act of 1935 met that day's social welfare expectations, it quickly became evident that America's changing economic environment had forced frequent patches to the act's core programs without upgrading and strengthening its economic and political base.

SOCIAL WELFARE POLICY DRIFT

Some may question whether there exists any public obligation to provide sufficient economic resources to reduce poverty and minimize its debilitating consequences, but an affirmation to do otherwise is more than a personal perspective. The Constitution of the United States declares this obligation, gives power to the Congress to implement it, and the US Supreme Court upholds the implementation of this obligation.[4] While there may be disagreement over the kinds of social products this obligation demands, and how these obligations are fulfilled, a commitment to provide at least some economic resources to those in financial need has been replicated throughout American history.

America's grudging willingness to act on behalf of the poor is companioned by a reluctance to confront structural issues that gave rise to poverty in the first place. Low wages perpetuate poor housing, dismally poor schools and forms socially negative behavior. An aversion to taxes, a free rider for the more affluent, denies government at all levels the capacity to resolve evident and nagging social issues. A disconnect between poverty and America's economic activities seems to emerge from deeply held negative beliefs about poor people, compounded by long abandoned philosophies about how the American economic and political systems function. Timeworn beliefs about capitalism, work, "free enterprise," and limited government activity all converge to create a political climate that is no longer consistent with the worldwide economic system of twenty-first-century America. An earlier political and economic system that respected requisite national social welfare architecture no longer survives to facilitate policy changes necessary to address poverty in today's idiom. Moreover, those who are motivated to live in a less poverty-stricken America fail to understand America's social welfare system as it exists today, not as it was created decades ago.

America has always approached poverty warily and with reservation. The relationship between America's obligation to respond to the problem of poverty among her citizens and her efforts to protect and promote "free enterprise" has been a source of tension since the beginning of the American experience. The tension goes to the very heart of the role of American governance. Certainly in times of economic crisis like the Great Depression and the Great Recession, America's obligation to her citizens outweighs her desire for an unregulated economic system. The economic compromises reached over the years have created a public/private balance that has satisfied the most egregious problems of poverty, while leaving the economy relatively free, but they have left a sizable portion of Americans still poor. The framework of this compromise rests on the misleading premise that as long as people work they will be protected from poverty. Historically, this is premise is not valid, and the most obvious lesson the Great Recession offers to America is that when jobs disappear, the social welfare programs fail.

The final chapter of this book argues that poverty in America only will be addressed successfully when the foundation of America's cash assistance programs are made appropriate to their twenty-first-century expectations. The Constitutional obligation assigned to America's social insurances under the framework of the Social Security Act provides the legislative authority and administrative capacity for a reformulation of cash assistance programs. The Chapter 6 conversation relies on several underlying assumptions: (1) The development of social welfare policy and programs under the authority of the Social Security Act over the past 77 years has led to social welfare fragmentation characterized by replacing poverty-reducing goals with ideological social welfare objectives. (2) Direct provision of cash does reduce poverty, as Social Security has proved. Poverty among the aged has been cut in half over the past 77 years due to changes in the Social Security benefit structure, but poverty for children has remained constant and is increasing. (3) With Constitutional grounding and legislative authority, two-thirds of the federal budget is spent on social welfare programs funded under the authority of the Social Security Act. This authority provides the best framework for reducing poverty in America. (4) Inordinate budget deficits in the present weak economy threatening America's social welfare commitments presents a prudent time to refocus the cash assistance programs more closely with poverty reduction in order to maximize the effectiveness and efficiency of federal social welfare spending.

A revised social welfare framework outlined in Chapter 6 may seem unfamiliar to some, unimportant to others, and insufficient for those who prefer more details than provided. At the same time, however, Americans are exposed to political debates that challenge the efficacy of the American social welfare system, and Americans seem much more amenable to reordering existing social commitments rather than large-scale social reform. Thus the proposals offered in Chapter 6 would refocus public resources on reducing poverty, deferring attention to details should agreement be reached on the larger objective. The review of America's experience with poverty, and our efforts to manage it, explain in large part the need to commit to a redirection of our resources before we decide the details of how to do it.

Part I Poverty: America's Shame ·∾·

1. Poverty's Elusive Heredity ❧

Give me your tired, your poor, Your huddled masses yearning to breathe free, the wretched refuse of your teeming shore. Send these, the homeless, tempest-tossed to me. I lift my lamp beside the golden door!

Emma Lazarus, *The New Colossus* (1883)

Strange that 130 years after this verse was written, and 110 years after it was enshrined at the Statue of Liberty, the golden door is tarnished, and now *our* shore is teeming with the tired, poor, and huddled masses yearning to breathe free. Young, old, women, men, and, sadly, children—as many as 25 percent of our children—have become America's twenty-first-century "tempest-tossed."

John Kenneth Galbraith's observations about American poverty more than 50 years ago sound familiar today:

> Poverty—grim, degrading, and ineluctable—is not remarkable in India. For few, the fate is otherwise. But in the United States the survival of poverty is remarkable. We ignore it because we share with all societies at all times the capacity for not seeing what we do not wish to see.... But while our failure to notice can be explained, it cannot be excused.[1]

America was a dream for those who came and still come, and many who freely came early did, indeed, realize their dream. Yet many did not. Industrialized America created urban slums equal to those the immigrants had fled; labor was exploited in the mines and on factory floors; children were fated to forced labor. There also were those who came involuntarily—African Americans who are still emancipating—and those who were already here that we conquered—Indians (Native Americans) who we forced onto reservations, and who live in deep poverty today. America has always had a large share of its people in poverty, and some critics continue to advise caution over efforts to do anything about it.

George Gilder, a well-respected conservative critic of American social welfare, advised,

> The moral hazards of current programs [to respond to poverty] are clear. Unemployment compensation promotes unemployment. Aid for Families with Dependent Children (AFDC) makes more families dependent and fatherless. Disability insurance in all its multiple forms encourages the promotion of small ills into temporary disabilities and partial disabilities into total and permanent ones. Social security payments may discourage concern for the aged and dissolve the links between generations....All means-tested programs (designed exclusively for the poor) promote the value of being "poor" (the credential of poverty), and thus perpetuate poverty. To the degree that the moral hazards exceed the welfare effects, all these programs should be modified, usually by reducing benefits.[2]

ANTECEDENTS TO PRESENT-DAY POVERTY CONCERNS

Judging from its long-standing prevalence and the sheer volume of literature, America has been obsessed with poverty, but it has not been willing to do very much about it. After all, America was presumed to offer the opportunity to *escape* poverty. Instead early immigrants found more of what they had supposedly left. Poverty in early America was so widespread that whole communities of workers rose up, spawning political activity that addressed the conditions of the poor. Confusions over what poverty is and what causes it have been dwarfed by unsuccessful struggles to reduce or eliminate it whenever poverty uprisings occurred.

Perhaps the first person to study poverty in a systematic manner was Amos Warner, an economics graduate from Johns Hopkins and one-time director of the Baltimore Charity Organization Society. In 1894, Warner studied 28,000 applications for "charity" (welfare) from which he developed two categorical determinants of poverty: "internal factors that included 'shiftlessness,' and 'lack of judgment,' and 'external factors' that included 'inadequate wages,' and 'limited education'," among others. Warner estimated that over 42 percent of all people seeking charity at that time were ill, "insane," or had other disabling physical defects.[3]

The ferment of the nineteenth-century social reform movement forced a number of structural social changes highlighted by the rise of organized labor, restrictions on child labor, and improved housing standards for working class poor. But as the financial rewards from increased productivity were passed down reluctantly to the poor, as political and social organizations began to engage actively in many structural issues related to poverty, such as poor working conditions, and as ideas of "Social Darwinism" gained prominence for explaining poverty, the social urgency to attack it gradually gave way to public economic optimism and a preference for social stability.[4] Gradually separated from its structural economic roots and tempered by political compromise, poverty lost its social urgency and instead developed as an ethical issue of personal failure, repulsive individual behavior, and family breakdown. The federal government reflected the nation's reluctance to become involved in poverty issues when President Pierce vetoed legislation sought by Dorthea Dix to extend federal land grants to states to care for the mentally ill in 1854.

Declining social concern over poverty was not only complicated by confusion over its character, but also by vague information about its extent. Although the first census took place in 1790, its purpose was strictly to count the number of American citizens for congressional apportionment. It was not until the 1850 census that there was any formal recognition of poverty in America. That census counted 66,434 "paupers" in 1849 who had been financially supported, wholly or in part, out of a total of 22 million residents. The census was not able to give a full account of additional people living in "poor houses," nor was it able to certify the number of paupers who might have received support from a large number of sources that were not registered as charities. Of course neither slaves nor Native Americans were counted as paupers. There was no estimate of the number of paupers who did not receive charity for various reasons; only those who received charity were counted. Yet this census did give attention to poverty in a limited way, and subsequent census counts continued to do so.

EMERGING FEDERAL INVOLVEMENT IN THE PROBLEM OF POVERTY

James Patterson's comprehensive history of America's extensive, complex, and frequently contradictory efforts to respond to poverty during the past 100 years certainly confirms America's ambivalence toward poverty.[5] Patterson notes that early twentieth-century social reformers began to infuse a national debate about poverty's social manifestations against a background of public discourse over personal characteristics that caused poverty. Patterson argues, perhaps correctly, that the social reformers emerged from a class of social and economic elites who undertook social reform as a method of preventing poverty to avoid direct spending on the poor. The social reformers, however, did lay a foundation for a national social welfare coalition that forced the federal government into hesitant steps that had significance for the development of the Social Security Act itself. These early social advocates varied in their specific political objectives, but they were united in their fervor to obtain the fruits of broad-scale social and municipal reform. While not always focused on the structural economic determinants of poverty the social reformers certainly drew attention to the plight of the poor early in the twentieth century and wrestled the federal government into several national undertakings. A political deconstruction of several high-profile federal government commitments the reformers achieved offers perspective on America's hesitant steps to engage with poverty. These early commitments reflect social welfare reference points as America continues to struggle to make today's social welfare endeavors more responsive to poverty.

Children: The creation of the Children's Bureau is arguably the first among several significant social welfare shaping events. The municipal and political reform movement, agitated by the growing suffrage movement of the late nineteenth and early twentieth centuries, focused sharply on the rights and welfare of children, highlighted by an unique White House Conference on Care of Dependent Children. At the behest of Lillian D. Wald, founder of the Henry Street Settlement in New York City, and her friend Florence Kelley, President Theodore Roosevelt agreed to call and keynote this 1909 Conference. Financial inadequacy was one of three forms of "dependency" discussed by the more than 100 conference participants. Julian Mack, a former judge of the Juvenile Court in Chicago closed the two-day conference asking, "How should we stop dependency?...Until we eradicate poverty, until social justice shall prevail we shall have dependents among us and therefore we must study best how to deal with them."[6] Yet there were no clear criteria for determining which children or their families were poor, let alone what to do for them.[7] One of the products from this Conference was the creation of the Children's Bureau in 1912 that was charged with collecting information about the welfare of children and recommending steps that could be taken to lessen their poverty.

The aged: The Children's Bureau provided the first national center for research and advocacy on behalf of children within the structure of the federal government, itself a precedent-setting event. The Children's Bureau had a profound impact on setting public policy on behalf of children and reducing poverty among them, at least up to 1996.[8] Although out of historical sequence, a similar example is provided by the formation of the Administration on Aging (AOA) in 1965 that followed a 1963 White House Conference on the Aged. Poverty among the aged was an important focus during the early years of AOA research and advocacy on behalf of the aged, and it contributed significantly to the development of Medicare in 1965, the 1972 changes in Social Security benefits that cut poverty among the elderly in half, and the Pension Reform Act of 1974 that established the Pension Benefit Guarantee Corporation to protect the value of private retirement pensions.[9]

Economic calamity: The Great Depression (circa 1929–34) certainly refocused the nation on poverty but in the context of large-scale economic collapse. The poverty of the Great Depression was viewed as a product of an economy that failed to provide jobs, and the early efforts of the Roosevelt administration was concentrated in creating jobs that would get people back to work. The Social Security Act of 1935 focused its attention on economic protection for the aged and unemployed who lost income when work was not available, and it also strengthened and standardized ongoing state efforts to provide financial assistance to the poor.

But achieving the Social Security Act rested on more than the prevailing economic meltdown. The social reformers had successfully badgered state governments to set up programs of welfare aid in their states, beginning with Illinois in 1903. By the time the social Security Act became law, every state had some mixture of state-funded public aid programs for children, the aged, the sick, and/or others who were considered financially needy in that state. In other words a national welfare architecture had begun to take shape, and the Social Security Act was able to rest a major part of its commitments on these widely diverse state welfare administrations. The social reformers also previously had worked assiduously to convince President Harding and the Congress to create a program of aid for mothers and infants with programs of mother and child hygiene and general public health care in 1920. Nor should the advocacy of Francis Townsend and the widespread politically influential Townsend group members be minimized when examining the development of Social Security itself. In other words the Social Security Act put in place pieces of a complex puzzle, which had been created by varied advocacy groups.[10]

Even though the Social Security Act did not deal specifically with poverty, it established a national social welfare architecture that addressed poverty marginally through programs designed to lessen personal

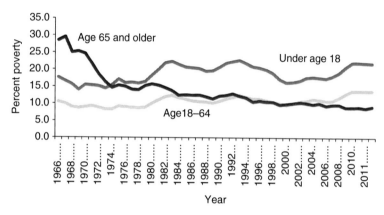

Figure 1.1   Poverty rates by age: 1960–2012
Source: Census Bureau Historic Poverty, 2014.

economic need. During the following decade a gradually improving economy assisted by the economic stimulus of WWII ushered in a time of American economic prosperity in which poverty continued to prevail, but it seemed politically irrelevant in the existing economic euphoria. Having a policy document in the form of the Social Security Act, however, allowed gradual expansion of programs, particularly Social Security, which progressively chipped away at poverty (see Figure 1.1).

Public recognition of poverty: With national income at peak levels, and with relatively full employment, Michael Harrington shook the gradual attrition of concern about poverty after WWII. Well before his galvanizing polemic *The Other America* was published in 1962, Harrington had been chipping away at America's indifference to poverty. His own religious experiences led him to the Social Gospel movement, and then to Dorothy Day and the Catholic Worker Movement, and then on to his socialist future. Along the way he discovered the "invisible poor" of the 1950s.

> The poor are politically invisible. It is one of the cruelest ironies of social life in advanced countries that the dispossessed at the bottom of society are unable to speak for themselves. The people of the "Other America" do not, by and large, belong to unions, to fraternal organizations, or to political parties. They are without lobbies of their own; they put forward no legislative program. As a group they are atomized. They have no face; they have no voice. Thus, there is not even a cynical political motive for caring about the poor as in the old days.[11]

Candidate John Kennedy was among those moved by Harrington's passionate call for the end of the two American nations (the Other America was the America of poverty). With the help of the Ford Foundation, Kennedy put in motion a political process that led to President Johnson's commitment to a War on Poverty in 1964: the Economic Opportunity Act (EOA). The EOA was the first national effort to recognize poverty, specifically: its elimination, or at the very least its containment, thus became a legitimate social welfare policy objective. President Johnson's design to eliminate poverty set it apart from previous initiatives to help poor people by creating a new set of social programs generated outside the authority of the Social Security Act and other existing social programs. These new programs were administered under the authority of a new administrative structure, the Office of Economic Opportunity (OEO), rather than the Department of Health Education and Welfare (so-named at the time). In addition, as the name illustrates, the programs themselves were focused toward providing economic opportunities for those in poverty largely through a service structure of self-help, vocational training, job placement, and better educational preparation to enter the workforce, rather than providing people with money.[12]

The public attention stirred up by the War on Poverty led to intense competition about which federal agencies would administer it. In an intellectual environment overwhelmed with theories, studies, and programmatic solutions, there quickly developed competitiveness for the new resources set aside for the War on Poverty among existing social welfare agencies. The decision to create a separate administrative unit, the Office of Economic Opportunity (OEO), irritated existing agency programs and threatened their financial support. Both the Departments of Labor and Health, Education and Welfare wanted a share of the "action," arguing that they were already confronting poverty through their existing services. Both lobbied heavily to become major program administrative agencies for the new Economic Opportunity poverty programs as they were being debated in the early months of the Johnson presidency. The working group that established the legislative framework for the Economic Opportunity Act rejected both agencies. The Department of Labor wanted to be the lead agency for the War on Poverty, but it had not demonstrated an ability to work effectively with the poor, and Secretary of Labor Willard Wirtz wanted to create new jobs for the poor while the president wanted to get the poor into existing jobs. The Department of Health, Education and Welfare had become too "categorical," and the working group feared that new initiatives would simply end up in old program packages.[13]

Eliminating poverty by creating economic opportunity was based on a theory of poverty that argued that by opening work opportunities for the poor, through education and training, the poor would find their way into jobs and begin to climb the ladder to economic self-sufficiency. Thus, while the War on Poverty focused serious national concerns about poverty itself, advocating for a battery of innovative services programs designed to open work for the poor contrasted with providing cash support for financially dependent people. James Patterson called this decision a "conceptual fuzziness" in OEO's diagnosis of poverty, adding,

> The contradiction is clear. If the poor included many who did not gain from economic growth—mostly people outside the labor market—then they probably needed handouts of some sort. The reluctance of planners to face that fact, and the refusal of Congress seriously to consider it, exposed again the resistance in America to costly programs that might sustain a permanent class of dependents on welfare.[14]

Hostile critics of government social welfare programs in general were quick to point out that neither cash assistance programs nor experience with Johnson's Great Society service oriented programs showed a measurable reduction in poverty or the nation's social problems. To the extent that the Great Society programs eschewed the use of cash assistance programs to "fight" poverty, some argued that the Great Society programs precipitated the wave of racial unrest of the late 1960s by setting expectations for social change without expanding welfare assistance to those who continued to be in economic need.[15] In retrospect, however, the Great Society programs did raise public awareness of poverty and economic need, and the entire Great Society enterprise was severely compromised, economically and politically, by the war in Viet Nam. With the exception of Head Start, the other War on Poverty programs either withered away or were integrated into programs operated by mainline administrative agencies such as the Department of Labor and the Department of Health and Human Services.

The federal government accepts welfare responsibility: The Supplemental Security Income (SSI) program was created in 1972 and first implemented in 1974. This was an important turn in efforts to reduce poverty because the federal government at last agreed to administer a national cash assistance program. Originally the cash assistance programs created under the Social Security Act, Aid to the Aged, Aid to the Blind, Aid to Dependent Children, and later Aid to the Disabled, were programs deliberately left to the states to administer with financial support from the federal government. As criticism of the War on Poverty mounted, before he left office President Johnson appointed the President's Commission on Income Maintenance, which concluded cash support was more important in fighting poverty than was generally appreciated, and called for "the creation of a universal income supplement program financed and administered by the federal government making cash payments to all members of the population with income need."[16] Contests over use of cash to reduce poverty existed from their very earliest initiatives, and the use of cash to eliminate it was promoted seriously as early as 1962 by the conservative economist at the University of Chicago, Milton Friedman,[17] and other conservative economists who believed a negative income tax would also be a more efficient way to relieve poverty than the existing system of state-administered welfare.[18]

By the time Richard Nixon became president, the War on Poverty had become a disaster,[19] and his domestic policy advisor, Daniel Patrick Moynihan, urged the new president to propose a new welfare policy to Congress, a Family Assistance Plan (FAP), which was patterned on previous economic and political ideas of a cash assistance program (see Chapter 4). Thus the idea of a "guaranteed annual income" (GAI) advocated by early conservative economists, proposed in the form of a "negative income tax" (NIT), was transformed into a family assistance plan (FAP); FAP became the centerpiece of the Nixon administration's welfare reform effort that he proposed to Congress (HR 1). The outcome after a prolonged political process was the creation of Supplemental Security Income (SSI).

SSI combined the Aid for the Aged, Aid for the Blind, and Aid for the Disabled into a single program of financial assistance paid for by the federal government. SSI set a standard federal payment, which states could supplement if they so wished, and it made this standard payment to everyone who qualified, based on their income. SSI income has had only a modest impact on reducing poverty because the eligibility level for a benefit was and is set well below the official poverty line. The significance of SSI, however, lay in the willingness and capacity of the federal government to assume full responsibility for a cash support program for the economically needy aged and disabled which it was unwilling to do in 1935 and for many years thereafter. SSI, however, did not extend its responsibility to financially dependent children, mostly for ideological reasons. The shift in this federal role for dealing with children in poverty is discussed further in Chapter 4.

A shift to family-based welfare: Temporary Assistance to Needy Families (TANF) represents the most recent milestone in America's effort to address poverty by shifting the public welfare needs of children to the private responsibility of the family. The Committee on Economic Security reluctantly included welfare programs in the Social Security Act, hoping their need would become unimportant as Social Security became more robust, but the need for SSI certainly exposed this illusion, cementing the federal government's commitment to welfare assistance. Unfortunately Congress could not bring itself to include children and their adult caretakers into the SSI program, and after years of struggling to find answers to the economic needs of poor children—establishing programs to enhance family stability, work incentive programs, tracking down "deadbeat dads" to get them to pay child support, setting up programs to promote marriage among single parents—Congress reformed Aid to Families with Dependent Children into TANF.

As far back as the 1970s, Senator Walter Mondale had been holding hearings on the family, urging a "family policy" as a basis of social welfare attention, and President Jimmy Carter, picking up the Mondale theme, promised to work toward developing pro-family policies and held a White House Conference on the Family in 1979.[20] The demise of the American family has been a constant theme throughout America's struggle with poverty, and the shift to family-centered social welfare is discussed more fully in Chapter 4. This shift was finally recognized formally when President Clinton set about to change welfare "as we presently know it," and TANF emerged from rancorous debate and contributed to a government shutdown before Congress finally passed this welfare reform.

The bitter struggle over cash assistance for dependent children signaled an enormous shift in child welfare policy. From before the Social Security Act was created, and subsequently firmly established within it, a strong commitment to provide cash assistance to poor children—and in 1959, to children in poor families—had existed since the founding of the Children's Bureau. By requiring parents to work as a condition for receiving cash assistance for themselves and their children, limiting the time a family could continue to receive cash assistance, and allowing states to penalize noncomplying parents by denying them assistance, the president and Congress allowed ideological poverty objectives prominence over objective economic needs. The work of decades that sought to eliminate and reduce childhood poverty was shattered by political partisan efforts to undermine fundamental objectives of New Deal social welfare.[21]

DEFINING POVERTY

In spite of these the high profile efforts engaged over the past decades in unsuccessful efforts to come to grips with poverty, there remains a residual disagreement about a poverty definition. In the early 1960s, the Joint Economic Committee of Congress estimated an annual family income of $3,000 or less as a poverty threshold, and the Census Bureau used this number in its discussion of poverty. Thus $3,000 became the poverty line for initial eligibility for OEO programs. In spite of concerns that a definition of poverty was more complex than setting it as a dollar amount, the War on Poverty sharpened agreement on a cash definition of what constituted poverty. However, Mollie Orshansky, a statistician in the Social Security Administration, pushed for a more flexible poverty definition that took into account family size and urged the adoption of the Department of Agriculture's "economy" food budget, multiplied by three, adjusted for family location and family size, with annual adjustments reflecting the cost of living, as the best way to measure poverty.[22] At first rejected by the Census Bureau and OEO, the Orshansky poverty measure became preferred by the Social Security Administration and has since been used as the official poverty measure (OPM).[23]

Concerns about the OPM, however, continued, and Congress funded a study by the National Academy of Sciences (NAS), Panel on Poverty and Family Assistance, which recommended a poverty measure that took into account various government programs and forms of in-kind resources. Its report, *Measuring Poverty: A New Approach*, was released in 1995. Based on this report, in March 2010, a Federal Interagency Technical Working Group developed a set of initial starting points to permit the US Census Bureau, in cooperation with the Bureau of Labor Statistics, to produce the supplemental poverty measure (SPM) that would be released along with the OPM each year. This SPM was not designed to replace the OPM, but to supplement it in order to give further clarity to a definition of poverty.[24]

Yet a third measure of poverty has been introduced in the process of studying poverty from an international perspective: a relative poverty measure (RPM). This measure counts the poor as those individuals with household income below some percentage of the median of that distribution. The typical resource measure is disposable household income that is equalized to control for variation in household size. The poverty threshold for this measure, then, represents the central tendency of a nation's distribution of financial resources, and poverty rates based on this measure provide information about the shape and size of the lower part of that distribution. A comparison of the three measures is provided in Table 1.1.

Interestingly, both the SPM and RPM show poverty to be greater than the OPM, according to Kathleen S. Short and the Census Bureau. Using 2011 as the benchmark year, the OPM measured 15.1 percent; the SPM

Table 1.1 Poverty measures: Official, supplemental, and relative

	Official Poverty	Supplemental Poverty Measure	Relative Poverty
Measurement unit	Families and unrelated individuals	All related individuals who live at the same address, any coresident unrelated children who are cared for by the family (such as foster children), and any cohabitors and their relatives.	Household
Resource measure	Gross before-tax money income	Sum of cash income, plus any federal government in-kind benefits that families can use to meet their food, clothing, shelter, and utility needs (FCSU), minus taxes (or plus tax credits), minus work expenses, minus out-of-pocket expenditures for medical expenses.	Disposable income
Poverty threshold	Cost of minimum food diet in 1963	The 33rd percentile of FCSU expenditures of all consumer units with exactly two children	50% median equalized disposable income
Threshold adjustment	Vary by family size and composition	Three parameter equivalence scale Adjust for geographic differences in housing costs using five years of ACS data	Square root of household size
Updating thresholds	Consumer Price Index: All items	Five year moving average of expenditures on FCSU	Annual update

Source: Kathleen S. Short, "The Supplemental Poverty Measure: Examining the Incidence and Depth of Poverty in the U.S. Taking Account of Taxes and Transfers in 2011." Washington, DC: US Census Bureau, December 11, 2012, p. 4.

measured poverty at 16.1 percent, and the RPM measured poverty at 18.2 percent.[25] The Census Bureau's comparison of the poverty rates for the year 2011 shows how the OPM and the SPM affect poverty populations differently. Because poor children receive medical benefits and some cash supplements under Social Security, their SPM is slightly lower than their OPM, but since the elderly have more medical expenses, their SPM is greater than their OPM (see Figure 1.2).

Elise Gould and Hilary Wething compare America's poverty incidence with peer nations using the RPM.

In the late 2000s, 17.3 percent of the US population lived in poverty—the highest relative poverty rate among OECD peers. The US relative poverty rate was nearly three times higher than that of Denmark, which had the lowest rate (6.1%), and about 1.8 times higher than the (weighted) peer-country average of 9.6 percent. While the overall relative poverty rate in the United States is higher than that of peer countries, the extent of child poverty is even more severe.... In 2009, the United States had the highest rate of child poverty among peer countries, at 23.1 percent—meaning that more than one in five

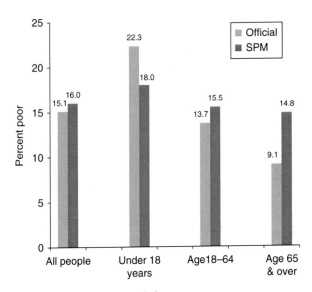

Figure 1.2   Poverty status by age and alternate poverty measures

Source: Kathleen S. Short, "The Supplemental Poverty Measure: Examining the Incidence and Depth of Poverty in the U.S. Taking Account of Taxes and Transfers in 2011." Washington, DC: US Census Bureau, December 11, 2012, p. 4.

children in the United States lived in poverty (as measured by the share of children living in households with household income below half of median household income). This level is almost five times as high as that of Iceland, which had the lowest level, at 4.7 percent, and over two times higher than the (weighted) peer-country average of 9.8 percent.[26]

SUMMARY

The highlights of America's past efforts to eliminate or contain poverty offer perspective for changing America's cash support programs in order to bring them up to twenty-first-century American social welfare needs.

Administrative presence: The experience of the Children's Bureau and the Administration on Aging show the importance of an administrative presence in the federal government capable of collecting subject specific information and articulating the income needs of the population it represents, both inside the administration and to Congress. The Children's Bureau was the incubator for the development of pre-Social Security Act financial assistance programs for children and provided a base for mobilizing public support for the Social Security Act during its legislative development. The Administration on Aging provided a nurturing political environment for Medicare and improved Social Security benefits for the elderly. Such agencies have great capacity for producing, collecting and analyzing information and provide a focal point in government for suggested policy changes.[27] The necessity of administrative advocacy has become an important element of both administrative and legislative policy development.

Significance of major economic events: The Great Depression provided the social and political energy that led to the Social Security Act, a major shift in American response to poverty. By acknowledging that widespread poverty was a result of structural economic failure "in this manmade world of ours," and creating a national architecture for dealing with poverty through its cash support programs, the Social Security Act has become the foundation for most of America's present energy to reduce poverty. The Social Security Act did not directly acknowledge a failed economic system as such, but it did recognize the fact that poverty is a problem of America's economic structure, and that the federal government has an obligation to respond with financial resources to address those affected by structurally induced economic need. The Great Recession has also demonstrated the failure of today's economic structure, exposing the inability of the present social welfare structure to deal with the individual consequences of this economic event. While the Social Security Act linked its response to the Great Depression by supplying work-related forms of cash support, the Great Recession is struggling with an economy that has lost jobs and a resulting cash support system that therefore ceases to function when there are no jobs.

Linking economics with social welfare: The Great Depression made possible America's first political linkage between its economic structure and social welfare. Until then, poverty was understood as personal failure within an otherwise independent economic system. But the events of the Great Depression modified existing perceptions of poverty. Later, the Employment Act of 1946 formalized a responsibility of the federal government to manage the economy in such a way that it would create full employment. The Social Security Act, the Employment Act, and the Economic Opportunity Act all emphasized the importance of jobs, and tied efforts to reduce poverty the ability to be employed and thus escape poverty. The Employment Act committed the United States to create a full employment economy and provided the ability to accept social welfare expenditures as a form of activity that aided, not detracted from, national development. Subsequently, a gradual political erosion of economic and social welfare affinity since the late 1940s, reflected in the atomization of social welfare commitments, as discussed in subsequent chapters, frustrates present efforts to make social welfare resources more amenable to efforts to reduce poverty. Considering the fact that the present cash support programs almost exclusively are tied to work, and that a full employment economy as anticipated by the Employment Act may not be possible until well into the twenty-first century, the events of the Great Recession challenge the foundation of America's present social welfare structure. The Great Recession made the linkage between economic and social welfare policy transparent.

Clarifying poverty: The War on Poverty offered two important landmarks in efforts to reduce poverty. First, it created an environment that at last forced an official definition of poverty as a lack of sufficient financial resources—a money definition. The large-scale objection to the Orshansky poverty measure, which continues to stand as the official poverty measure (OPM), has led to the creation of two related poverty measures—the Supplemental Poverty Measure (SPM) and the Relative Poverty Measure (RPM)—but both maintain financial insufficiency as their base. The SPM is now used as a comparison to the Orshansky measure, as shown above, and interestingly enough, while the SPM provides greater nuances in defining poverty, its conclusions are similar to the OPM.[28] The SPM provides an alternative to the OPM, particularly for identifying those elements of cash support programs that might have the best chance of reducing poverty for specific populations. An official definition of poverty not only makes it possible to measure poverty over time, but its financial adequacy base anchors the poverty definition.

Second, the War on Poverty demonstrated the limitations of reducing poverty through a service strategy focused on private sector jobs. Getting the poor into the labor force, particularly as it is structured in twenty-first-century America, is much more complex and expensive than the War on Poverty expected, and even if possible, the War on Poverty demonstrated that work itself is not sufficient to eliminate poverty. The EITC developed after the failed work strategy of the War on Poverty obliges the federal government not only to give tax credits to low-income employees, but also to provide them with a cash supplement, further clarifying poverty as financial dependency, not as a work deficiency. Thus, EITC epitomizes a fundamental structural economic problem. As in the case with TANF, even with the high energy needed to get low-income people into jobs, it is far from certain that jobs alone will lift people out of poverty without accompanying cash assistance and a variety of in-kind services. Since EITC subsidizes low-paying jobs, without any compensation from low-wage employers, it supports an argument that the present economic structure cannot absorb people living in poverty without a form of public cash support.

Poverty's ideological burdens: Throughout the history of America's attempt to deal with poverty, those efforts have been burdened by ideological issues originating in nineteenth- and twentieth-century beliefs and attitudes. Most are fiction, but they persist in part because they provide justification for protecting the nineteenth- and twentieth-century structures of American capitalism. It is simply not true that the poor do not want to work, but the myth supports suppression of wages at below-poverty-level wages. The ideological issues attached to the creation of TANF simply have forced parents into sub-poverty jobs and children into poverty. It may be impossible to do, but successful efforts to reduce poverty must shed the ideological baggage attached to it.

As America has discarded its grand effort in the War on Poverty, and as the OPM and the SPM have become official poverty measures of the Census Bureau, the Congressional Budget Office, and nongovernmental policy centers such as the Brookings Institution, the Center for Budget and Priorities and the Institute of Poverty, the experiences of dealing with

American poverty have led to a greater understanding of American poverty and how it can be managed, reduced and eliminated. Poverty is not a static condition of ne'er-do-wells. Half of those in poverty rotate in and out of it during the course of any year. Many individuals and families remain in poverty less than a year, but over 40 percent are in "deep poverty," meaning that they are not only very poor but also less likely to escape poverty at all. Children under age five, African Americans, female-headed families, and sick and disabled people all are most likely to be poor. The federal government has become the source of efforts to reduce poverty, yet it has no agency within the administration or in Congress that focuses interest and resources to reduce poverty. Present cash support programs are widely scattered through America's political and economic infrastructure. Poverty-reducing efforts continue to be riddled with ideological barriers attached to their availability. While good political fodder, ideological objectives produce little in the way of reducing poverty and lead to intensifying cultural misunderstandings of poverty in America's rapidly expanding cultural inclusiveness.

CONCLUSION

Poverty in America's Twenty-First Century

Economic Policy Institute authors Lawrence Mishel, Josh Bivens, Elise Gould, and Heidi Shierholz conclude their recent study of poverty by arguing, "Economic growth and poverty reduction clearly became decoupled in the mid-1970s, just as income inequality was taking off. As income inequality grows, poverty rates become less responsive to overall growth, because too little of that growth reaches the lower end of the income scale."[29] They continue,

> During the most recent full business cycle, 2000–2007, rising inequality of U.S. incomes...contributed more than any other factor to...the increase in the U.S. poverty rate....In other words, controlling for changes in racial, educational, and family structure composition, had income growth been more broadly shared over this period, poverty would have hardly increased from its most recent low in 2000. From 2007 to 2010, inequality continued to play the most significant role, though falling incomes also increased the poverty rate.[30]

Poverty for everyone except the elderly seems to increase as income disparity grows (see Figure 1.1).

As income inequality grows, poverty rates become less responsive to overall growth, because too little of that growth reaches the lower end of the income scale. Therefore, economic growth is a necessary factor in, but not *sufficient* for, broadly shared prosperity. The way economic growth is distributed becomes a crucial factor in understanding persistent poverty. While the US economic system might be the engine that creates economic growth, its political system provides the pathway over which the growth is distributed. The political economy of poverty is much more multifarious than trying to fix poor people.

America's economy has changed over the past century, but it still insists that poverty is an individual problem. Looking at its long arc, abounding with efforts to reduce or eliminate it, suggests that poverty has become endemic to the American economic and political systems, regardless of how poor people may be viewed. With the exception of poverty among the aged, the percentage of people in poverty has remained constant during the past 50 years. As the country has become richer, and as the population has expanded, the relative amount of poverty has remained about the same. At the same time, during the past several decades, and culminating with the Great Recession, the distribution of financial resources in the United States has grown more unequal. In 1968, the richest quintile of earners collected 43 percent of all the income generated in the United States, but in 2010 this richest fifth of the population collected 50 percent of all income. America's richest 5 percent of all earners received 27 percent of the income! According to the Congressional Budget Office, the Gini coefficient for market income inequality now stands at 0.59, up from 0.37 in 1997.[31] It is hard to say that America's political and economic systems have become more effective at reducing poverty. Poverty need not persist in America.

The demographics of American poverty as illustrated in Appendix 1.1 suggest a complex relationship between personal and structural poverty that is difficult to deconstruct. Clearly poverty is clustered in definable demographic groups. Children, female-headed households, African Americans, Hispanics, renters, and those without private health insurance are more likely to be poor. Efforts to reduce American poverty have for the most part focused on these clusters, with efforts designed to help those in poverty become more like their counterparts in similar demographic groups who are not poor. Such efforts must contend with the facts that the clusters overlap one another, and it in some cases, the direction of relationship between a particular demographic group and their poverty status is unclear. Are people poor because they are renters, or are they renters because they are poor? Are people poor because they have no health insurance, or do they lack health insurance because they are poor? Children may be poor because they are African American, or they live in female-headed families, or they may also be poor because their parents cannot afford private health insurance needed for a serious medical event.

The above questions are not simply rhetorical, or deliberately designed to make the discussion about poverty ambiguous. The political history of American poverty has favored modifying the behavior of poor individuals, with the expectation that changed behavior will change their poverty status. For example, the fact that certain behaviors, like teen pregnancy, correspond (correlate) with a particular poverty cluster does not determine whether teen pregnancy creates poverty or whether poverty causes teens to become pregnant. Nor does this relationship help deconstruct the observation that many pregnant teens do not end up in poverty. Certainly the truth of the matter lies with both the individual teen and the economic structure in which the teen finds herself. Social science now has at its disposal massive amounts of social data and sophistical statistical procedures capable of finding relationships between poverty and an ever-extending list of personal characteristics. Fashioning a model of specific personal characteristics that, if corrected, would reduce poverty, therefore, has become meaningless, if not useless.[32] A lack of money, on the other hand, is the single factor shared by all those in poverty.

The political history of poverty is not meant to suggest that everyone who is poor must be given money. It does seem prudent, however, to examine what it is about America's economic, political, and social structures that contribute to the depth and the pervasiveness of poverty in the most economically advanced nation in the world. If poverty is the inevitable result of advanced economic development, then perhaps giving money outright to the poor would certainly be justified, and there are strong arguments for this conclusion. Nor are the above questions raised to minimize the fact that public and private spending on behalf of poor people definitely has benefited those in poverty. In spite of these efforts, American poverty persists. Moreover America has developed a complex and far-reaching social welfare scheme that, too, has become ineffective at reducing pervasive poverty, and the above observations are not meant to call for increased spending to reduce poverty, although given the way income and wealth are distributed in America, such a call would also justified.

The following chapters are designed to provide broader perspective on these concluding thoughts about poverty in America and how it can be contained. American poverty requires a restructured social welfare system. With the gradual ending of the War on Poverty programs, America no longer has a public policy document or federal administrative agency specifically directed to reducing poverty. The cacophony of efforts to explain poverty has led to simplistic conclusions that creating a program aimed specifically at one or another "cause" would remedy it, a conclusion not justified by America's experience. Yet, America has cash support programs in place that can be reconstructed to provide the kind of economic security Americans deserve and that will lead to a reduction of poverty. These social welfare structures, however, will require rebuilt foundations attuned to the vicissitudes of the economic system in twenty-first-century America. This is the theme of the following chapters.

The next chapter explores the ideas behind America's economic system, not the specific the economics of it but how it operates with respect to the social welfare commitments America has made. The themes that follow in subsequent chapters join pre-twenty-first-century economic, social and political assumptions recognized as the failure of the American economy to meet today's economic expectation, with a shrinking ability of the existing social welfare system to protect Americans from structural economic changes. America's cash support programs have been stretched incrementally to meet changing social welfare demands, but they remain fixed in foundations no longer relevant in today's political and economic environment and thus are incapable of meeting their expectations and reducing poverty.

The final chapter proposes that the cash support programs be brought together under the authority of the Social Security Administration, a politically ambitious proposal but one that notes the existing cash programs are interconnected. While this conclusion may not seem very far-reaching it argues forcefully that such consolidation will provide a twenty-first-century political and economic base for American social welfare as America reshapes its economy.

2. A New Capitalist Order Needs a New Social Welfare Mandate ✋

A merica's economy scorns poverty. The most robust economy in the world sustains one of the highest rates of relative poverty among all industrialized nations, but America spends less than 16 percent of its Gross National Product (GNP) on social programs—less than 17 other comparative nations.[1] America ranks last of 27 developed nations in the percentage of reduction in poverty from tax and transfer programs; America has the largest percentage of children in poverty of all industrially developed nations—over 20 percent of America's children are poor. Worst of all, economists Mishel, Bivens, Gould, and Shierholz state, "Despite the relatively high earnings at the top of the U.S. income scale, inequality in the United States is so severe that low-earning U.S. workers are actually worse off than low-earning workers in all but seven peer countries."[2] While not disputing those individual personal failures that might cause poverty, certainly, the American economic system seems ill-equipped to deal with poverty in a substantive way, compared with other advanced economies.

America's economic undertakings and its social welfare initiatives are frequently discussed as discrete entities, yet both are entangled. Both the present economy and the existing social welfare system were created and are perpetuated in the context of pre-twenty-first-century realities, and both are given form by a political system based on the same seventeenth- and eighteenth-century assumptions. Thus, both America's economic system and its social welfare arrangement each are expected to function beyond their founding structural capacities. The Great Recession exposed structural flaws in America's system, provoking calls for reforms that will prevent future damaging economic events. "The U.S. economy needs to be restructured in directions that are not yet clear. What is clear is that it will take resources, and it will take public spending," says Joseph Stiglitz.[3] The Great Recession exposed America's social welfare flaws that need restructuring as well, and that, too, will take resources and public spending. Pre-twenty-first-century economic, social, and political building blocks explain the failure of both the American economy to meet today's economic expectation and the inability of the existing social welfare system to protect Americans from structural economic disaster. These same structural flaws have prolonged poverty over the course of the past 50 years.

THE FOUNDATION STONES OF AMERICAN CAPITALISM AND SOCIAL WELFARE

Historian Sean Wilentz observes that American democracy "developed piecemeal, by fits and starts" with conflicts over politics and economics often at the centers of the debates. "The conflicts of the twentieth century...are more likely to see economic power and interests as the matrix for politics and political institutions. For Americans of the early republic, politics, government and constitutional order, not economics were primary to interpreting the world."[4] Economic interests have looked beyond poverty as if economic growth would obviate an orderly social welfare development to deal with it. Incremental economic, political, and social adjustments such as those made after the Great Depression of 1929 and continuing to the present for the most part have been layered over historic and social and economic canons. While America's economic system has moved beyond its old rules, America's social welfare commitments remained fixed in historic, economic, political, and social doctrines. Regardless of how it is named, America's present-day social welfare enterprise did not suddenly appear with the Social Security Act in 1935. Rather it grew out of the way long-held economic preferences and political purposes played out in America's changing social environment.

American Capitalism in Perspective

It would be a mistake to suggest that America's economic system developed from a set of economic rules independent of its surrounding social and political context any more than to assume that America's social welfare enterprise developed exclusively from proverbs of Christian charity, yet both grew from the same roots. In 1989, the well-respected social economist Robert Heilbroner[5] (1919–2005) wrote a short piece for *The*

New Yorker explaining the growing influence of capitalism in developing nations in contrast with receding forms of socialism and communism. The success of capitalism as an economic form, Heilbroner argued, had prevailed because "capitalism is a social order, based upon deeply embedded and widely believed principles...an order of life, a regime" founded on two authority centers in American life: "the 'economic' prerogatives of the 'business system,' [and the] 'political' prerogatives of the governmental system."[6] Heilbroner argued that capitalism is a fundamental system of economic and political thoughts.

If Heilbroner's conclusions are accurate, the US economic system, usually called capitalism, has melded a blend of eighteenth-, nineteenth-, and twentieth-century economic, political, and religious beliefs into distinctly American economic dogmas from which capitalism continues to operate. A collision of these historic economic building blocks with twenty-first-century political, social, and economic realities challenged both "the economic prerogatives of the business system and the political prerogatives of the governmental system" with major and minor consequences for their economic security and financial well-being.

Capitalism's economic (business) birthright: America's present-day understanding of capitalism[7] no doubt begins with Scotsman Adam Smith (1723–90), and the context from which he wrote is important in order to understand what he wrote because it was different from the context in which Smith is esteemed today. Smith was a product of the early eighteenth-century Enlightenment, which emerged from a gradually more prominent role for science over an earlier system of beliefs. It was a period of time when people asserted their ability to reason and thus discover the "immutable laws of nature" on their own. Such reasoned discoveries challenged time-honored religious teachings and existing forms of governance. It was a time of rising individualism, when people began to affirm their own personal uniqueness. This Age of Enlightenment, a period of emerging understanding through human reasoning, provided the intellectual context in which Smith lived and the economic and political climate in which he wrote *The Wealth of Nations* in 1776.[8]

Smith began writing from his background in moral philosophy[9] and the influence of his older good friend and intellectually skeptic, fellow Scotsman David Hume. Smith seemed to begin by accepting Hume's premise that humans were born with sympathy for others, something akin to empathy or a general benevolence, and that everyone behaving in their own self-interests would balance out in the best interests of all. In this context, Smith relied on the idea that brought pursuit of individual economic self-interest into harmony with sympathy for others, thus creating a more harmonious social order than those established by authoritarian edicts. *The Wealth of Nations* (1776) emerged from this context and Smith's experiences during time spent in France.

While there, Smith observed the value of agricultural labor that produced tangible products, and he began to see a distinction between productive and unproductive labor. Productive labor, like farming, produced things. Unproductive labor, such as English mercantilism, created nothing. Smith argued that productive labor was the source of national wealth, and if productive labor was left alone, the self-interest of each person would encourage others to create more products, and in turn, the benefit to one person from the creation of more products would accrue to the benefit of the whole of society. Smith argued that if the individual economic exchange of products were left to take place without government interference, self-interest would be limited by competition through the processes of the exchanges. In this natural environment, national wealth would grow, and the betterment of each laborer in the pursuit of self-interest would lead to the betterment of all through this system of personal, free exchanges, later called "the invisible hand."[10] Much later, neoclassical economists identified the outcome as "economic equilibrium," where available supply matched available demand through a free exchange of goods and services. The mechanism of this process was the "market," the substitute for the invisible hand.

This highly selective synopsis undeniably is unfair to Smith and *The Wealth of Nations*.[11] It is a gigantic work, not only in its length, but also in its scope. Smith discussed economic subjects from labor to the use of money and political subjects from forms of governance to respect for the sovereign. He mentions the plight of the poor, particularly taxes on labor that disadvantage the poor, for example, and he laid the groundwork for discussing the politics of economics, which he calls "political economy." The sheer breadth and depth of Smith's magnum opus has encouraged selective summaries such as that above, particularly by latter-day neoconservative economists. Individual, unrestricted economic exchanges, however, seems to be Smith's major theme.

Milton Friedman (1912–2006) perhaps stands as the twentieth-century's most successful advocate of classic economic thought that emerged from the work of Adam Smith. While he sought to repudiate the emerging Keynesian economic theories, and although most of his academic writing pursued a better understanding of monetary policy, Friedman's influence fashioned a neoconservative school of economic thinking that gained widespread economic and public policy support. *Capitalism and Freedom*[12] provides the most accessible entrance to Friedman's larger economic philosophy. Cautioning against an intimate connection between economics and politics, Friedman argues that very survival of American democracy builds on his argument for "a *free private enterprise exchange economy*—what we have been calling competitive capitalism" [Friedman's emphasis].[13]

Friedman also claims, "The kind of economic organization that provides economic freedom directly, namely competitive capitalism, also promotes political freedom because it separates economic power from political power and in this way enables the one to offset the other."[14] Government is necessary to make sure the free private exchange economy functions smoothly, according to Friedman:

> In summary, the organization of economic activity through voluntary exchange presumes that we have provided, through government for the maintenance of law and order prevent coercion of one individual by another and the enforcement of contracts voluntarily entered into, the definition of the meaning of property rights, the interpretation and enforcement of such rights, and the provision of a monetary framework.[15]

Critics of classic economics point out that there must be competition free of monopolies and perfect information if neo-capitalism theories are to prevail. Nor do neo-economic ideas leave room for economic externalities where the full cost of a product is not included in its price. Allowances for these and other practical economic issues were addressed by extending Smith's theories to meet everyday economic realities and provide much of the framework for present-day neoconservative economic thought that drives many contemporary American economic practices.[16]

Perhaps the most problematic feature of Smith's ideas and their subsequent embellishments arises from Smith's assumptions that individuals and individual firms are the actors in the competition that leads to equilibrium. This view concluded that aggregating individual decisions would explain the structure of the entire economy, or in other words, that the whole is a sum of its individual parts. The early economic ideas assumed that individuals or individual firms could act independently and make their own free choices without consideration of those factors that determine or limit an agent and his or her decisions. Simply adding up how individuals behave does not determine the group behavior, nor are individuals free agents unconstrained by social and political exigencies. These two economic caveats also have important social welfare significance. Poverty, for example, is not a monolithic condition but made up of vastly different individual experiences, and the free agency of a poor person is constrained by social, political, and economic restraints.

Capitalism's political heritage: Politically, American capitalism rests on a laissez-faire government foundation. This is minimalist, "That government is best which governs least," kind of government based on Lockean liberalism fashioned into a political form by James Madison and defined by a constitutional state, toleration by multiple communities, and the protection of private property. Implied in the American constitutional state is a limitation of personal freedom in exchange for the assurance of freedom of all under the laws of a "social contract," individualism that requires toleration since individual beliefs cannot be fused into a single belief system, and protection of property that emerges from an ascetic understanding of labor. Individualism is the source of private property. "Whatsoever, then, [each person] removes out of the State that Nature hath provided, and left it in, he hath mixed his labor with and joined to it something that is his own and therefore makes it his Property," according to John Locke.[17]

Madison fashioned both American Federalism[18] and political checks and balances deliberately to prevent government from becoming too great a force in people' lives, or the rise of a political oligarchy. He feared that "factions" of self-interest would overwhelm the governmental process and assert their self-interest on others. Thus Madison urged increasing the number of "factions" (enlarge the Republic) rather than trying to limit their influence in the belief that the self-interest of one would neutralize the self-interest of another, thus reflecting a view not inconsistent with that of Adam Smith. To further restrain the influence of factions, Madison created the system of checks and balances, in which one branch of government is limited in its ability to assert its influence on the other branches, an important addition to Montesquieu's theory of separation of powers.[19] Madison admitted this arrangement would frustrate considerable government initiative, but he felt that was appropriate, as he also believed that government had to be restrained.[20]

James MacGregor Burns refers to the Madison solution as deadlocked democracy.[21] American government's reluctance to adjust "private enterprise" for the public good is inherent in a political structure of interest groups and checks and balances, resulting in a moving borderline between public sector governance and the private sector. Public sector governance assents to legal protection of private sector economics. Laws safeguard private property. Private property is secured by the Constitution and cannot be claimed by the government without "just compensation." Patents and copyright laws shield inventions. Corporations and their shareholders receive special tax protection.

American democracy, like American capitalism, is a compromise of eighteenth- and nineteenth-century beliefs that define a particular form of democratic government—one that balances a high premium on individualism on the one hand with the need for governance on the other. Other democratic forms of governance such as parliamentary systems differ not only in structure, but also in their founding principles and may provide more or less governmental latitude to deal with fundamental economic issues. While there are a variety of economic theories that explain personal and collective economic activity, the early nineteenth-century theories of Adam Smith, enthusiastically refurbished by Milton Friedman and other economic neoconservatives in the past several decades, make a good fit with America's limited government. The notion that the pursuit of self-interest will lead to the well-being of all, through unfettered self-adjusting economic markets, melds well with a form of government valued for its limited capacity to promote specific economic objectives.

America's ethical legacy: It is difficult to define American capitalism independent of American beliefs that favored classic economic thought as outlined above. While there are many sources of belief systems that shaped America's economic and political institutions, perhaps none are more important than America's Protestant religious beliefs. All economic systems rest on work as the foundation for individual sustenance and national growth, but work in the system of American capitalism is more than an economic necessity. Work in America is a moral requirement: a work *ethic*. Americans may talk blithely about someone who has a good work ethic or a bad one, but deconstructing this phrase reveals a deeper meaning of work in America.

Max Weber proposed that American capitalism developed as a particular blend of personal and social ethics forged by the religious teachings of Protestantism. Weber deconstructed America's transformation of work as a moral principle by examining the dictums of Benjamin Franklin: "Truly what is here preached [by Franklin] is not simply a means for making one's way in the world, but a peculiar ethic. The infraction of its rules is treated not as foolishness but as forgetfulness of duty. That is the essence of the matter. It is not business astuteness, that sort of thing is common enough, it is an ethos."[22]

Poor Richard's Almanack, a collection of annual events, biblical references and Franklin's own proverbs published regularly from 1733 through

1758 reflect Calvin's ethical burden on work. Franklin's Richard might be poor, but if he worked hard God would not let him starve. On the other hand, "if we provide encouragement for Laziness, and support folly, may it not be found fighting against the order of God and Nature which perhaps has appointed Want and Misery as the proper Punishments for, and Caution against as well as necessary consequences of Idleness and Extravagancy."[23] Work governed all ordered conduct for the early American capitalists, Weber argued, and anything, such as "impulsive enjoyment of life [which led] away from both work as in a calling or religion was as such the enemy."[24] And as strange as it may sound to the ears of American capitalists today, early capitalists valued the work, not how much money the work produced. Of course it is not hard to see how capitalist values shifted from how hard one worked to the money work produced, since the two were tightly woven together. Lacking a moral ethic behind hard work, however, money, not hard work, has become the preferred capitalist objective.

This simple explanation of work as a defining principle of American capitalism does not take into account why people do not have adequate personal resources, or whether work itself provides enough resources to meet personal needs. The moral imperative forces people to work regardless of the characteristics of the work itself. America's work ethic not only preserves capitalism's economic character, but it also provides justification for the accumulation of capital. It is impossible to build capital without work (by someone), and capital is needed to create work. Thus the antagonist argument goes: The surplus from the work of all must go to the needs of some who do not work, and thus deprives the community of further work opportunities.[25]

In summary, these deeply embedded principles of American economics, governance, and ethical behavior support an economy of freedom from government regulation that operates for the betterment of all through an invisible hand. A political system with divided centers of authority immobilizes centralized government decision-making, and private property is enhanced by a moral allegiance to work. Today of course American capitalism operates outside these principles on a day-to-day basis exposing capitalism's many paradoxes and leaving it vulnerable to changing social, economic, and political events, as it surely has. Only the foolish would seek to adjust today's realities to yesterday's principles, and the Great Recession verifies the fallacy of economic efforts to do so.

America assigns pejorative labels to those economic endeavors not founded on the same suppositions as American capitalism. For example, government-driven economic forms may be called "socialist" or "communist" because they do not reflect prevailing American economic, political, and ethical assumptions. It seems unacceptable to Americans that government should replace free enterprise as a framework for economic activity. Yet, even when labels are given to particular economic systems, it may be impossible to find pure examples of any of them. American governance, for example, does place limitations on "free markets," and it uses its taxing and spending authority to stimulate various forms of economic activity; yet the American economic form is still recognized as capitalism. While it may be unfair to call American capitalism a philosophy rather than an economic system, it remains difficult to understand American capitalism apart from its strictly economic manifestations.

Joseph Schumpter, for example, understood capitalism as an ongoing form of economic activity depending on an evolving social and political environment in a state of constant change due to the introduction of new consumer goods, new and more efficient methods of production and transportation, the constant opening of new markets, and new forms of industrial organization. Schumpter writes,

> The essential point to grasp is that in dealing with capitalism we are dealing with an evolutionary process.... Capitalism then is by nature a form or method of economic change and not only never is, but never can be, stationary. And this evolutionary character of the capitalist process is not merely due to the fact that economic life goes on in a social and natural environment which changes and by its change alters that data of economic action.

Schumpter forecast that capitalism would eventually give way to socialism because strong ideological differences existed between capitalism, as economics, and democracy, as a form of government, which could invoke unsolvable conflicts between government and business: "From the first standpoint the results [of capitalism] reads that the means at the disposal of private interests are often used in order to thwart the will of the people. From the second standpoint, the result reads that those private means are often used in order to interfere with the working of the mechanism of competitive leadership."

At least until the present time, however, American governance has been successful in adjusting the economics of capitalism to minimize such conflicts, even to the extent of partnering with private interests, thus preserving capitalism's basic character, but forfeiting a vigorous competitive democracy.[26]

Paul Krugman[27] provides a little less sanguine explanation for the dominant role a form of capitalism plays in many economies today. Underscoring recent international developments of more participatory governments, such as the collapse of the Soviet Union and modernization in China, Krugman argues "capitalism is secure not only because of its successes—which...have been very real—but because nobody has a plausible alternative.[28]

Although there is a vast literature on capitalism and the significant elements of America's economic system, America's present economic system, however named or however structured, is not a static structure, but an arrangement of economic pieces subject to change as present social and political realities challenge it. It is unproductive if not impossible to define American capitalism precisely as economics because the characteristics that make up America's economic system are constantly in a state of unrest, and as the flaws in the present American form of capitalistic way of doing things have become clearer, American government has often acted to shore up its version of capitalism in the face of its shortcomings. Yet America's economic developments still maintain ties to their economic, political and ethical history.[29] Putting new wine into old bottles has consequences as the Great Recession illustrates.

CAPITALISM AND AMERICA'S SOCIAL WELFARE EXPERIENCE

The above discussion explains in part the peculiar development of American social welfare, which has been reluctant to confront poverty. An American economy cemented in individual initiative, fragmented government power, and a moral imperative to work left little space for a structure to accommodate the poor or a political system necessary implement one. Poverty was an individual issue. Buttressed by the academic fad of Social Darwinism, the poor were people who just could not make it: Sorry!

The Great Depression (circa 1929–35) broke the barriers, however. The classic economy had crashed. There were no jobs. Government was forced to do something. Given this context it is not surprising that the first thing the Roosevelt administration did was create jobs in order to put people back to work. This significant departure from laissez-faire economics marked an important redirection for American social welfare. For the first time in its history the federal government stepped in and used public resources to protect individuals from the effects of a failed economic system. The Social Security Act signed into law by President Roosevelt in 1935 established a unique social welfare landmark. It created two new social welfare systems: social insurances and a national system designed to provide financial aid to states so that they could carry on their basic work of providing welfare assistance to those in financial need.[30]

But in spite of this break with the past, the Social Security Act remained cemented in eighteenth-century economic, political, and ethical thoughts. The distinction between social insurance for those who had work attachment, and providing welfare assistance to the needy who could not work, was deliberate.[31] Social Security and Unemployment Insurance remained well within traditional economic values under the guise that both were "earned" through previous work, a rather narrow view of social insurance. Although federal funds for welfare assistance required states to set standards for benefit payments, they had no effect on the structure of welfare aid to the poor. They simply provided federal funding to states for the welfare programs states had traditionally offered.

The fact that Social Security began its expansion toward a less stringent work-connected program almost immediately did not alter its underlying economic suppositions. Extending benefits to female spouses of retired workers maintained the principle of workforce attachment through their work-eligible spouses. The fundamental mechanism that ensured a work attachment for Social Security was the payroll tax. The payroll tax promoted individual economic self-sufficiency in old age by mandatory contributions to a government managed retirement fund. It also cemented its political stability for the next 75 years.[32] Financing unemployment insurance, too, maintained its workforce requirements. Only those who had worked, and worked for specified periods of time, were granted unemployment insurance, and the program made clear that the unemployed had to be registered and looking for work in order to continue to receive benefits. Paid for by the federal government and left to the states to administer, in many ways unemployment insurance was crafted less to provide financial relief for the unemployed, and more as a means of getting the unemployed back to work. Thus the Social Security Act left the economic system in the same place as it was before the Great Depression.

Employment Act of 1946

Keynesian economics introduced a new set of principles that challenged the game rules of American capitalism. The British journalist and financier John Maynard Keynes (1883–1946) departed from nineteenth-century economic theories by arguing that governments had the capacity to achieve a robust economy through their taxing and spending powers. In other words government was not a laissez-faire economic player; instead government was the invisible hand. Observing that spending supported a strong economy, Keynes made little distinction between whether spending was public or private as long as the spending led to employment, for in the final analysis a fully employed population kept the economy growing through its spending.[33] The Keynesian breakthrough in economic thought, however, added to, rather than replaced, most eighteenth- and nineteenth-century economic principles.

Paul Krugman notes,

> Since the time of Keynes, economics has been split into two subdisciplines. Microeconomics, the study of how individual firms, households and markets behave, is a field that operates by fairly strict intellectual rules. Firms are assumed to maximize profits, households to maximize their consumption. Market outcomes are carefully deduced as the 'equilibrium' that results from the interacting decisions of rational economic agents. Meanwhile, macroeconomics, the study of the business cycles, inflation and unemployment is full of ad hoc assumptions that, in the jargon of the field are not 'derived from microfoundations.'[34]

A neoconservative "synthesis" forged an uneasy blend of historic economic beliefs with Keynesian principles arguing that macroeconomic planning simply realized former economic principles. This synthesis abandoned pleas for completely "free" markets in exchange for entreaties on economically feasible, limited government economic management. Work in order to achieve full employment, however, remained central to both neoconservative and Keynesian economists.

The nuances of Keynesian economics are more comprehensive than this simple statement, and while this new economic thought had little specific effect on Roosevelt's New Deal programs, it finally worked its way into American politics when Congress passed the Employment Act of 1946. The act went through a tortuous political process. First proposed in 1945, it contained language that guaranteed a right to employment and an obligation on the part of government to provide sufficient resources to assure "continuing full employment."[35] Business interests fought the bill fearing the rising strength of labor unions, and when it was reintroduced in 1946 the provisions that guaranteed jobs for Americans were removed to in order to ensure its passage.[36]

The Employment Act of 1946 provided the nation with the tools for macroeconomic planning and the authority to implement taxing and spending decisions in order to promote economic growth. According to Julian Zelizer, American governance always understood that government taxing and spending affected the larger economy, but until 1946, government lacked the authority to use its taxing and spending power to influence the direction of the economy: "The postwar period was different. Income-tax policy was used as a macroeconomic tool through which expert officials could stimulate national economic growth or restrain excessive expansion."[37]

The Keynesian economics of the employment act opened the door to approaching social welfare in a different way. The adoption of Keynesian economics offered a synthesis of America's economic system and America's social welfare commitments, both seen previously seen as separate aggregated systems of individual (microeconomic) activity. Now, social welfare taxing and spending became macroeconomic tools. Spending for unemployment insurance, for example, was viewed as an economic stimulus tool, and the Social Security payroll tax was viewed as an encumbrance on economic growth. Thus both Unemployment Insurance, and to a lesser degree Social Security (retirement) were seen as more than programs to help individuals who needed cash support. The Employment Act and the Keynesian thinking that drove it put social welfare spending in the center of economic planning where it had not been before.

The Employment Act of 1946 laid the foundation for today's fiscal policy by creating three new structures: First, the Council of Economic Advisors prepares yearly reports on the conditions of the economy for the president, with recommendations of measures that would achieve the requirements of the act. Second, the act requires the president to report annually to Congress on the state of the economy, based on that report. Third, the act created the Congressional Joint Economic Committee (JEC) and charged it with obtaining information necessary for Congress to carry out the purposes of the act, thus giving Congress new and expanded economic authority. Although the substance of reports from both the Council on Economic Advisors and the Joint Economic Committee has been varied, macroeconomic discussions have always recognized social welfare and particularly the social insurances as issues in national economic planning.

It is important to note that shortly after it was formed, the JEC began to study poverty. In 1949, JEC created a Subcommittee on Low-Income Families that began a series of studies on the low purchasing power of families with incomes less than $2,000 per year. JEC continued its review of poverty programs and issues over the next several decades, concluding with its 20-volume *Studies in Welfare*.[38] This series of documents stimulated interest and research from more than 100 leading scholars and policy experts who provided public information about individual social welfare programs and included comments on their economic consequences. The series of studies constituted one of the most comprehensive reviews of the macroeconomic significance of programs designed to reduce poverty, and it still stands as a major contribution to the literature on poverty's structural issues. Much of this information has been reviewed and reevaluated by contemporary scholars and provides the base for considerable discussions about social welfare and poverty today.[39]

KEYNESIAN ECONOMICS AND SOCIAL SECURITY

Once it became evident that social welfare indeed had fiscal consequences, Keynesian economics began to play a part in the development of America's social insurance programs as they were put into practice, although not as a means to enhance their value. Social Security, in particular, was designed to build up its financial reserves in order to make it actuarially sound "in perpetuity."[40] As the trust funds began to grow, however, Congress questioned the wisdom of large government reserves. Martha Derthick reported that the Social Security Trust Funds began growing as early as 1937. Republican Senators, and Senator Arthur Vandenberg in particular, opposed amassing government reserves in the Social Security Trust Fund, for fear of excessive government spending and the risk of undermining private investments.[41] Both Roosevelt and Morgenthau reluctantly gave in to the rising tide of Keynesian economics that favored government spending rather than building government reserves by rejecting scheduled payroll tax increases. Eric Patashnik noted that Keynesians objected to Secretary of the Treasury Henry Morgenthau's insistence on large Social Security Trust Fund reserves, arguing that large reserves would drain private money out of the economy; Congress agreed and severely reduced the projected fund balance. "This was accomplished through an expansion of benefit payments and the cancellation of a scheduled payroll tax increase—policy moves that Keynesians strongly approved of."[42]

Macroeconomics, therefore, has plagued Social Security from its very beginning, and confusion over financing has been Social Security's frailest link with the public. Clearly the funds collected from yesterday's workers have not been set aside for today's retirees, although most Americans think this is the case. Social Security's architects were aware that Social Security would not be solvent "in perpetuity" as Roosevelt initially insisted, and both he and Secretary Henry Morgenthau succumbed to economic pressures: keeping payroll taxes low, tacitly allowing benefit expansion, and approving "borrowing" Social Security funds, all consistent with an economic philosophy designed to avoid a large buildup of government financial resources, while currying political favor with the elderly.

Macroeconomic planning established the capacity of American politics to accommodate to new economic challenges, but it has done so without corresponding support to accommodate the new demand placed on America's social welfare commitments. Social welfare programs therefore were forced to develop incrementally, as if the larger economic decisions had no significance for the way they developed. Instead social welfare expansion was driven by administrative preferences without sufficient economic authority to support them in the long run. The social welfare growth discussed in the next chapters remained fixed in their historic, economic, political, and ethical origins. The Employment Act, for example, revered the virtue of work, but failed to give authority to government to create it. The act promoted the counter-cyclical value of cash social welfare programs but did nothing to make Unemployment Insurance and other cash assistance programs more accessible during economic downturns.[43] The Keynesian limited preference for spending as a means for economic growth allowed a political fairytale vision of Social Security financing, placing a heavy financial obligation on today's workers. Over and over again American fiscal policy has favored tax reductions over public spending, and "the link between economic and social policy thus has been largely coincidental."[44]

Ideologically, American social welfare remains trapped in a commitment to capitalism's eighteenth- and nineteenth-century individualism, free markets, and the *work ethic* as the foundation of its policies, while on the other hand American government is committed to regulating free market activity in order to foster economic growth, achieve economic balance, and promote economic justice. The ideological and political disconnect between macroeconomic commitments to develop the larger American economy and the financial needs of individual Americans become evident in the long-standing spending debates that play economic development against social welfare spending.[45]

THE CALL FOR A NEW ECONOMIC ORDER

By most accounts, the American economic meltdown that began in 2008 has been the worst economic disaster since the Great Depression of 1929–35. This crisis would have been even greater were it not for some of the economic safeguards put in place after the Great Depression and a variety of social programs that had been created over the years to cushion the economic impact of such events on individual Americans. According to Joseph Stiglitz, "The current crisis has uncovered fundamental flaws in the capitalist system."[46] At the same time, various social programs fell far short of protecting Americans from the devastating results of its economic collapse.

Stiglitz argues that not only had the neoclassical economic model failed to anticipate the Great Recession, but it also failed to remediate the situation once it became evident that the economy was crashing. Instead, stabilizing the economy took great infusions of federal dollars into the economy, most of which had to be borrowed, and few of which went to support individuals who were caught in its vortex. Not only does Stiglitz eviscerate neoclassical economic arguments as a framework for the American economy of the future, but he also notes a growing schism in Keynesian economics between those who favor less government intervention and those who favor more. Stiglitz takes a vigorous government intervention view; he argues that a new capitalist order requires moving beyond the obvious financial crisis, usually blamed for the Great Recession, and using the resources of government to redirect the economy without losing the economic vitality of the private sector. Accommodations to preserve vestiges of capitalism are not new in American history, nor is there novelty in a vigorous application of Keynesian economics to achieve a better functioning American economy. America has the economic strength and the political authority to move the economy in a new direction; America also has the economic strength and political authority to develop to move its social welfare commitments consistently with its new economic order, but it remains tethered to its earlier principles.

The need for a new economic order has profound consequences for America's social welfare obligations, particularly those capable of providing cash to the poor. Stiglitz reflects on what has become more transparent. America's manufacturing economy has shifted to a service sector economy; the global economy has a massive underutilization of human resources, beginning with unemployment problems in the United States.

Productivity gains in manufacturing have been achieved by applications of technologies at the expense of labor. The distribution of income and wealth has become more unequal with money going from those who would spend it to those who already have more than they need. Finally, individualism plays a smaller role in American economic life. As Stiglitz argues,

> The model of nineteenth-century capitalism doesn't apply in the twenty-first century. Most large firms don't have a single owner. They have many shareholders. Today the main distinction is that the ultimate owners the shareholders in one case are citizens operating through a variety of public agencies and the other they are citizens operating through a variety of financial intermediaries, such as pension and mutual funds, over which they typically have little control. In both arrangements there are significant "agency" problems arising from the separation of ownership and control: those who make the decisions neither bear the costs of mistakes nor reap the rewards of success.[47]

Each of these social and political changes that call for a new capitalist order suggests the need for an accompanying new social welfare order as well. For example, Stiglitz points out the solvency of Social Security, as we know it today, depends on long-range actuarial forecasts that in turn depend heavily on the amount of employment, wages, population shifts and longevity. Almost exclusively tied to the payroll tax, five years ago the Social Security Trust Fund increased by $179 billion, but in 2010 it increased by only $92 billion.[48] Dependence on the payroll tax—which in turn depends on work and wages—has produced wide fluctuations in solvency, which depends upon macroeconomic events that Social Security cannot control. Ample evidence suggests that with 58 million people receiving Social Security in America today, and with almost another 6 million Americans receiving Unemployment Insurance in February 2013, there is an undisputable need for America's social insurance programs. But whether they should be tethered to work or developed as part of national fiscal policy has not been seriously considered at this point, in spite of the recognized need for changes in America's economic system.

A CALL FOR A NEW SOCIAL WELFARE ORDER

Recurring flaws in America's capitalist system have profound effects on America's social welfare system as the above Social Security example suggests. The economic changes Stiglitz documents portray an ideology that values individualism, but a system where individualism has become largely absent. Economic self-sufficiency has become a myth, and the relationship between work and economic success has become nebulous at best. Finding and holding employment is likely to be determined less on personal qualities and work habits but more on amorphous decisions made by "the firm." Unemployment is likely to be the result of fewer jobs due to global employment outsourcing and technological advances made in industry rather than lazy welfare recipients. Even as a countercyclical program, Unemployment Insurance had little impact on the overall economy during the Great Recession and proved inadequate for protecting the unemployed from serious financial losses.[49] The Great Recession exhausted precious personal savings, making older people subject to retirement with vastly limited resources. The social insurances, Social Security and Unemployment Insurance, ensconced in their eighteenth-century framework, proved an inadequate cushion for the new kind of economic forces Americans experienced.

Without question, things would have been much worse were there no Social Security or Unemployment Insurance, but these two social insurance programs proved incapable of reaching those who were rapidly falling off the economic ladder. For example, it is true that Unemployment Insurance claims rose as the recession deepened, but limitations in the program forced many off the program as their benefits became exhausted as the recession continued and deepened. Moreover, the effects of benefit exhaustion were uneven across the nation since each state has its own state-specific criteria for determining Unemployment Insurance eligibility.[50] The 2012 federal extension of unemployment benefits (P.L. 112–96, February 2012) narrowly missed defeat as congress squabbled over unrelated budget issues, and Congress refused to extend the benefits into 2014, only to provoke more Congressional squabbling over whether they should be extended further.

Even with its expanded scope, Social Security could not mitigate the personal economic challenges presented by the Great Recession. While some employees who lost jobs probably decided to apply for early Social Security benefits,[51] these were people who already had built some Social Security benefits sufficient for early retirement, but such early retirement resulted in reduced monthly benefit amounts. Those who chose not to retire early, or were not eligible for early Social Security retirement, were denied Social Security credits during their unemployment spell. Particularly for those who had jobs covered by Social Security, but remained unemployed for an extended period of time, loss of Social Security wages will reduce their benefits when they do retire. The Great

Recession undermined the economic structure of Social Security itself. As an economic stimulus, President Obama was able to secure a one-year payroll tax reduction of 2 percent for employees for 2010,[52] but this meant that approximately 13 percent of OASDI Trust Fund income ($87.7 billion) had to be taken from general treasury funding to reimburse the Social Security Trust fund.[53]

These ongoing funding shortcomings are understandable because both Social Security and Unemployment Insurance are tethered to work. When there is no work for people, no benefits are forthcoming. Putting people back to work, therefore, is not only an issue of economic growth, but it is also a social welfare issue of eligibility for social insurance benefits.[54] If there is no work, people are forced on to the welfare programs. These welfare programs, Supplemental Security Income and Temporary Assistance to Needy Families proved to be even less adequate than the insurance programs, and financial eligibility thresholds for these programs is so low that they had little economic protective value. Moreover, these programs are "discretionary" programs requiring yearly Congressional appropriations, and no increase in appropriations for these discretionary programs has been authorized during the Great Recession. In fact, these are the very programs that are being reduced as the 2013–14 budget "sequester" continues.

Clearly the Great Recession has challenged not only today's economic system, but also the social welfare programs and very foundation upon which they rest. Perhaps most significantly, the economic failures of the Great Recession exposed the flaws in America's social welfare system that account for America's inability to reduce poverty over the past half-century. Chapters 3 and 4 analyze how both the insurance and the welfare (cash assistance) programs have outgrown their eighteenth- and nineteenth-century foundations. These programs can no longer provide the kind of economic protection for Americans for which they were created. Because today's social welfare programs are so dependent on work, they are trapped in a larger economic system that has changed dramatically, allowing poverty to persist and failing to provide economic security for millions of Americans during this recent economic meltdown. The final chapter outlines what must be done to protect Americans from personal economic collapse in future years, during the call for a new social welfare order consistent with America's new capitalist order will continue. Yet, as important as it is to protect Americans from personal economic disaster with a more effective social welfare system, the most important failure of American social welfare has been the damage caused to the entire country by an inadequate social welfare structure, an increase in poverty, and the creation of an income gap between the top and bottom that is greater than it has been in the past 50 years.

CONCLUSION

Joseph Stiglitz sounds the alarm that income disparities have threatened American democracy:

> Real democracy is more than the right to vote once every two or four years. The choices have to be meaningful. The politicians have to listen to the voices of citizens. But increasingly, and especially in the United States, it seems that the political system is more akin to "one dollar one vote" than to "one person one vote."[55]

If social welfare must remain a measure of American capitalism, then both must face the forces of change and adjust accordingly. Capitalism in the United States has always been a product of the culture, with some economic suppositions fitting better than others. Governance has developed to assure a political climate that maximized an economic form believed best suited to an ideology consistent with its political structure. However, when the crisis of the Great Depression forced the Roosevelt administration to push the nation beyond the established social welfare policies of that day, it did so assiduously, keeping its innovative (for the United States) social insurances well within the established thresholds of capitalism as it was then practiced. Now, as the Great Recession forces Americans to think about a new national economic form that retains some of its nineteenth century rudiments adjusted to Keynesian propositions, it behooves Americans to review the social welfare system in light of its changed structure. More than ever before, as American governance exercises more authority over the national economy, social welfare, particularly the social insurances, require a renovated foundation.

Perhaps unwittingly, when Congress passed the Employment Act of 1946, it validated the obligation of our government to manage the nation's economic and social welfare activity, and repudiated laissez-faire economics. The powers given to Congress with the original Employment Act have been expanded into the present-day complex capacity of the federal government to control almost every aspect of the American economy, a process called "fiscal planning" today. The political choices to use this capacity sparingly, and in many cases not to use it at all, were primary causes of the Great Recession. Critics of government's failure to act, such as Stiglitz and Krugman, not only criticize government for its ineffective regulatory actions, but also for its failure to use its taxing and spending power, long the basis of Keynesian thought enshrined in the Employment Act and its expanded authority over the past 65 years.

In spite of eighty years of grudging changes, the economic and political foundation of America's social welfare programs remains grounded in nineteenth-century suppositions while the nation now operates on a twenty-first century infusion of Keynesian principles. The mismatch of economic progress on the one hand and social welfare development on the other has recently expressed itself in political gridlock, and continued poverty is the consequence of this incongruity for millions of Americans. As an example, the social welfare system failed to protect the private property lost by individual homeowners, driving many into poverty, while national fiscal policy protected corporate private property of large-scale organizations. The inability to respond to individual human need in the face of economic collapse exposed a social welfare system anchored in values of self-sufficiency through work in an economic environment where work itself no longer ensures personal economic independence. America's economic system has been forced out of its nineteenth-century neo-capitalist residence and into an American twenty-first-century idiom, and it must take its social welfare commitments along with it if there is any hope of success in reducing poverty.

Part II   The Cash Support Programs: New Wine in Old Bottles ❧

3. The Social Insurances ❧

INTRODUCTION

The Social Security Act was created in 1935 as America was emerging from the Great Depression. Revisiting this monumental legislative achievement 80 years later arouses nostalgia not unlike visiting a childhood home. It may be the same basic house, but it may have an addition or different windows, and it may even look a bit shabby. It often seems smaller. As comfortable as it might have felt in childhood, the home seems insufficient for one who has grown up and faces present day realities. Returning to a childhood home causes change: a change in the environment and a change in the way the past is remembered.

Pondering America's childhood social welfare home also generates a struggle between yearning for the past and a recognition that the past, as comfortable as it may have been, no longer suffices for today's social welfare realities. The Social Security Act was a large and comprehensive document by that day's standard, consisting of 12 parts that introduced a relatively untested American experience of government-financed social insurance, and it consolidated a wide array of social welfare programs that had been financed by and unevenly scattered throughout individual states. It created America's first comprehensive social welfare structure.

Eighty years ago, America's childhood social welfare home seemed quite adequate; today an alternation here and there may have changed its appearance somewhat, but its basic foundation is still the same. The original 12 parts of the act have grown into 21. Medicare and Medicaid, a limited form of government-financed health care, have been loaded onto the original Social Security Act without any modifications to its original structure. The foundation of America's social welfare childhood home is simply too small to hold up under the burdens layered on it over the years. It may look different, but it still sports an 80-year-old framework.[1]

Conservative political spokespeople have been trying to disassemble America's social welfare structure almost since its beginning.[2] They argue that social welfare does not belong in the economic neighborhood of American free enterprise, that it tramples individual private property rights, and contaminates America's economic environs with people who do not work. At each juncture of challenge and confrontation, liberal political advocates have rescued America's basic social welfare structure with incremental modifications and program additions that fundamentally expand its scope but are incapable of making important changes to it creaky, overstressed original foundation. The Great Recession exposed a top-heavy social welfare construction stretched well beyond its origins, rendering it incapable of undertaking what it was established to ensure: "financial security against the economic hazards and vicissitudes of life."[3]

Maybe this comparison of the Social Security Act with a childhood home becomes a little unreal, but a reasoned critique of America's social welfare programs in the wake of the Great Recession concludes that they have been made inadequate for America's twenty-first-century obligations, beginning with the social insurances. Because of their narrow base in the Social Security Act, America's social welfare commitments do not target poverty; instead, they reflect the widening gap between rich and poor, placing a greater burden for social welfare on the middle class. These social welfare obligations fail to take into account that the nature of work has changed, and they fail to recognize that the very nature of the American economy has changed as well. Nowhere are these shortcomings more evident than in the social insurance programs that were designed to protect income when work is lost.

The Social Insurances

Social Security and Unemployment Insurance are the most extensive and most expensive of all of America's social welfare programs.[4] Both programs anchored the original Social Security Act as America's first comprehensive social welfare undertaking. As noted in Chapter 2, these two social insurance programs broke with traditional social welfare endeavors by protecting income for the aged and unemployed when they were not able to work. These programs were created not as "welfare" programs, but as "entitlement" programs with rights to their benefits politically guaranteed through their previous work. Social Security guaranteed an entitlement to benefits even more firmly since employed workers (and their employers) contributed to a trust fund from which these benefits were paid. The creation of this national program of social insurances, a long-resisted American idea, represented a politically expedient effort to bring immediate financial relief to those who lost work-related income without a welfare stigma.

Those who developed the Social Security Act gave scant attention to broader social goals—like insuring spouses or children— nor is there evidence that the American pioneers of social insurance had much vision about where such social insurance initiatives would eventually lead. Economically, neither program pretended to confront poverty, nor, since benefits from both programs were based on earned wages, below-poverty-level benefits were just an unavoidable outcome of the programs' structures. Since the social insurances were tightly knotted to work, they were supported by the economics of nineteenth-century capitalism. With unemployment at unbelievably high levels during the Great Depression, this system of social insurance emphasized work, personal self-sufficiency, and minimum government involvement, particularly in the case of Unemployment Insurance. The Social Security Act never set out a comprehensive social welfare design; it simply reflected an accommodation of America's existing social welfare activities to the ideology of nineteenth-century capitalism, with work as default requirement to obtain both Social Security and Unemployment Insurance benefits.

Social Security

Social Security was and is the prominent cornerstone of America's social welfare structure. Today 58,586,000 people—more than 18 percent of all Americans—who include retired workers, spouses, children, mothers and fathers, widows and widowers, receive an average monthly Social Security benefit of $1,186.60 (see Figure 3.1). By any measure, Social Security is America's largest public investment.

Social Security was developed on three fundamental work-related principles: First, benefits were restricted to retired workers who contributed (paid taxes), provided they had worked a specified period of time.[5] Each worker had (and still has) his or her own Social Security account from which benefits were (and are) computed. Second, benefit amounts were calculated in relation to earnings. Those who earned more received higher relative benefits. Finally, Social Security would be sustainable in perpetuity, that is permanently, financed by worker contributions in the form of payroll taxes. These contributions would be socked away in a trust fund until they were needed to pay benefits. Although Social Security was established on these founding principles, today's American workers more or less accept it as the modified program it has morphed into.

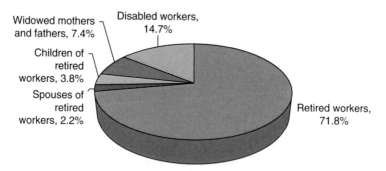

Figure 3.1   Percentage of Social Security benefit payments (total monthly benefit payments: $65,918 million)

Source: Social Security Administration, Monthly Statistical Snapshot, May 2014.

Social Security today has expanded well beyond its original intentions. If it had followed its founding principles, its financial crises would never have happened. Instead, social and economic contingencies have forced Social Security out of its original sheltered environment, but its founding premises remain the same.

Beneficiary changes: Over the course of its history, an enlargement of Social Security's beneficiary base has stretched it well beyond its original purpose. The 1935 law only allowed retirement benefits to the primary worker. But within 4 years, a 1939 change in the law added survivors' benefits and benefits for the retiree's spouse and children. Since then, it has been modified every year, sometimes more than once. Congress has revamped Social Security over 42 times, with more than 334 different major program-changing amendments. Included are 31 changes to the categories of beneficiaries, and 11 discretionary increases in the amount of benefits until they became automatic in 1975.[6] Appendix 3.1 tracks the 31 major beneficiary changes since 1935, and all but one of those changes expanded the beneficiary pool. Those receiving Social Security have expanded well beyond the original conception of individual retirees, or even the 1939 decision to benefit family members. Today, retired workers make up only about two-thirds of Social Security's beneficiaries.

While most of Social Security beneficiary expansion took place without a corresponding change in the fundamental structure of the program, the expansion of Social Security to include Disability Insurance in 1956 provides an important exception. Congress resisted simply adding a new beneficiary group to the then existing program. Instead the benefit expansion to include the disabled necessitated a structural addition to the basic program. This came about because the 1948 the Advisory Committee on Social Security recommended that it should be expanded to include those who became physically disabled and unable to work. Congress, however, declined to expand the program's beneficiary pool. Subsequent Advisory Commissions continued to recommend that the beneficiary pool be extended to include disabled people, and Congress finally agreed to do so in 1956, but with accompanying changes to Social Security's structure. Instead of simply expanding the beneficiary pool to include disabled people, Disability Insurance was created as a separate program entity under Title II of the Social Security Act. Disability Insurance required funding by a separate payroll tax earmarked to a separate trust fund, and administered by a separate set of rules.[7] The specific program change, however, did not alter Social Security's basic work-related benefits principles.

Benefit levels: Inconsistent benefit levels paid to recipients have vexed Social Security. Although originally a provision existed to increase the Social Security payroll tax rate, there was no provision to increase benefits as the cost of living increased. Thus benefit levels remained fixed until 1950 when Congress amended the Social Security Act to provide a whopping 77 percent increase. In subsequent years, Congress continued to adjust benefit levels 8 times, sporadically, and at its discretion, with little reference to increases in cost of living and scant attention to Trust Fund balances. As the frequency of these increases and the amounts of the increase became a political tool to curry favor with the elderly, particularly in election years, Congress decided to establish automatic benefit cost of living adjustments (COLAs) based on the Consumer Price Index in 1972, with the first automatic benefit increase taking effect in 1974. While COLAs are essential to preserve the value of Social Security to the beneficiary, benefit increases were not met with a change in the structure needed to pay for them. Sometimes the payroll tax was increased and sometimes it was not. Thus improved benefit levels were advanced without consideration of Social Security's original financing structure, placing an unanticipated future financial burden on the program.

Patricia P. Martin and David A. Weaver called the 1970s "a watershed decade in [social security] program history." General benefits increased by 15 percent in January 1970 and by 10 percent in January 1971. Legislation in 1972 provided another 20 percent increase in benefits. A separate piece of legislation enacted that year increased the basic benefit rate for aged widow(er)s from 82.5 percent to 100 percent of the deceased spouse's benefit—in essence, a permanent increase of 21 percent in the benefit rate, beyond the general increases applying to all beneficiaries. In addition, in 1972, policymakers created a special minimum benefit, which was designed to help long-term, low-earning workers.[8] Chapter 2 explained how economic choices designed to minimize the size of the Trust Fund allowed most of these beneficiary changes.

Benefit adequacy: The low level of benefit payments has hobbled Social Security. Although President Roosevelt only expected Social Security to provide approximately one-third of a retiree's income, low-earning recipients' payments were often so low that they were eligible for welfare along with their Social Security. Amendments to Social Security in 1939 established a formula for calculating benefits designed to provide relatively higher monthly benefits for people with lower earnings compared with those with higher earnings. Benefit "progressivity," a form of income redistribution integral to the program almost since its beginning, damaged the principle of benefits based on wages. Social Security was designed as a guaranteed benefit insurance program, not unlike private sector insurance or annuity programs. In the case of Social Security, however, the benefit guarantee is determined by applying a formula to the total earnings after they are "indexed" or brought up to financial date. The formula for 2013 is shown in Box 3.1. By altering the formula, as has been done almost every year since Social Security was created, the distributional elements have been increased. Early recipients benefited greatly by the formula used to set benefits, while subsequent formula changes have produced less progressive benefits over the last decade.[9] Today lower earners still receive approximately 12 percent of their lifetime wages from Social Security while high earners receive approximately 2 percent less than their lifetime wages. As desirable as such redistribution may be for social welfare policy in general, it certainly deviates from a main principle and puts a particular burden for income redistribution on Social Security.[10]

Social Security's economic sustainability: As discussed in Chapter 2, sustaining Social Security has always been one of its most contestable features. Originally, the program sought to meld financing practices of private insurance into a public system built around an earmarked tax and a separate fund to hold these taxes for further use: the payroll tax and the trust fund. Problems with this arrangement were apparent almost immediately, as the payroll tax generated a large amount of revenue, and the trust fund grew in size, as benefit outlays were small. Thus large reserves were created, which, in a private insurance system present little problems, but large government surpluses create macroeconomic issues. Government can do little with large financial surpluses that have large growth potential and must be held for several decades.

Fiscal juggling also has contributed to Social Security's unsustainability. As discussed in detail in Chapter 2, Keynesian economists argued that large trust fund reserves constituted a lock box of otherwise private capital, and they were likely to advocate for pay-as-you-go financing. Robert Meyers, the Social Security chief actuary, was a master of actuarial forecasting, and he followed the more traditional approach first argued for by Henry Morgenthau, President Roosevelt's Secretary of the Treasury. The early tax and benefit adjustments of Social Security's first few years quickened when Wilbur Mills joined the United States House Ways and Means Committee in 1942, just as congress was struggling with its new found authority as a result of the Employment Act. Mills was a quick study in tax matters, and by the time he became chairman of this powerful committee in 1957, he had become one of Congress' most adroit tax experts.[11] The complexity of Social Security taxing and spending was presumed too difficult for members of Congress to understand in order to vote intelligently, and thus Mills insisted on a closed rule when the committee brought Social Security matters to the full House for a vote.[12]

Mills found a partner in the Social Security Administration who disagreed with Meyers' full funding approach. Wilbur Cohen worked as a researcher for the Committee on Economic Security beginning in 1934, and he steadily moved up the administrative ranks until he became the agency's Congressional legislative liaison. Soon he began working closely with Mills on Social Security issues.[13] Mills' desire to manage the size of the trust fund[14] coincided nicely with Cohen's interest in broadening Social Security into a more comprehensive social insurance program, which lead to the greatest beneficiary expansion in the history of Social Security (see Appendix 3.1). Expanding the beneficiary pool kept the size of the trust fund below the economic radar, and correspondingly, expanding benefits kept American social welfare policy conveniently aligned with the then generally favorable treatment of the elderly. Juggling deferred payroll taxes with increased benefits resulted in 11 years in which the Social Security program did not generate enough revenue in FICA taxes to pay that current year's benefits, forcing it to draw on its trust fund reserves.

The payroll tax contributed to unsustainability in two other ways. First, the payroll tax presumed to establish the principle of each worker contributing to his or her retirement fund, but as noted in Chapter 2, it was more important for its political backing than its economic value. Second, payroll taxes were protected from general revenue use and locked in a Trust Fund. This has led to countless arguments as to whether the protected Social Security funds were a government asset or a liability in the development of the federal budget each year. Since the size of the Trust Fund has been manipulated by the ever-changing social Security payroll tax rates, its existence is more economic fiction than reality.

While the initial payroll tax was quite modest, the fact that it was tied to workers' wages made it inherently unstable. High employment and strong wages, as was the case after WWII, would produce large revenues; conversely, a slow economy would drain resources needed for future retirees. Forgoing scheduled payroll tax increases to keep reserves low or to stimulate economic growth only contributed to the instability of the payroll tax as Social Security's funding source, particularly in times of extending the beneficiary pool. The inconsistent changes to the rate of taxation differed significantly from the orderly progression of tax increases Roosevelt demanded in the original Social Security Act.

Although Roosevelt insisted that Social Security be completely financed by those due to receive the benefits, his own Committee on Economic Security anticipated the infusion of general revenues by 1980, causing Roosevelt to insist that the actuarial tables be corrected in order to make Social Security sustainable in perpetuity. It never happened. Over the ensuing years, three streams of general revenues entered Social Security financing: one after WWII to cover veterans who had no Social Security coverage while they were in service; another in 1972 when benefits were expanded to provide adequate benefits to retired people age 72; and a third in 1983 when amendments to the Social Security Act taxed benefits, and subsequently returned the taxes to the trust fund. A fourth steam of general revenue entered Social Security in 2011 when President Obama secured a 2 percent payroll tax reduction as an economic stimulus plan. This temporary reduction in the payroll tax rate reduced payroll tax revenues by $103 billion in 2011 and by a projected $112 billion in 2012. The legislation establishing the payroll tax reduction also provided for transfers of revenues from the general fund to the Trust Funds in order to "replicate to the extent possible" payments that would have occurred if the payroll tax reduction had not been enacted. Those general fund reimbursements comprised about 15 percent of the program's noninterest income in 2011 and 2012.[15]

BOX 3.1　COMPUTING SOCIAL SECURITY BENEFIT PAYMENTS

For an individual who first becomes eligible for old-age insurance benefits or disability insurance benefits in 2013, or who dies in 2013 before becoming eligible for benefits, his/her PIA will be the sum of:

(a) 90 percent of the first $791 of his/her average indexed monthly earnings, plus

(b) 32 percent of his/her average indexed monthly earnings over $791 and through $4,768, plus

(c) 15 percent of his/her average indexed monthly earnings over $4,768.

We round this amount to the next lower multiple of $.10 if it is not already a multiple of $.10.

Source: Social Security Administration.

According to Dalmer Hoskins, America's almost exclusive reliance on payroll tax financing of Social Security places the United States outside the practices of most industrialized countries that have long used general revenue funding to supplement payroll taxes and other forms of earmarked taxes in their social security programs. In France, Germany, and Japan, general revenues fund 30 percent to 50 percent of public pension program expenditures. Hoskins suggests that America's reliance on the payroll tax largely has been a political decision, not an economic one, based on a political reluctance to raise taxes. Other industrialized nations have built legitimate social objectives into their programs, worthy of being financed not only from individual worker and employer contributions, but rather from general taxation. America's expanded Social Security financing remains firmly anchored in the payroll tax.[16]

Social Security summary: The inability of the basic structure of Social Security to support its program changes, and the efforts to reform it without dealing with its basic structural shortcomings, might be best summarized by the work of the 1983 Greenspan Commission, appointed by President Reagan. The financial stability of Social Security was called into serious question after the 1977 amendments failed to stabilize its finances. In spite of assurances that funds would remain adequate in the near term, with anticipated surpluses in the 1990s and early 21st century, increased inflation and lowered wages led to projections that by July 1983 revenues and trust fund assets would be inadequate to pay benefits in the forthcoming 15 years. Thus, 5 years after Congress "stabilized" its finances, the president was forced to appoint a new commission charged with a "major overhaul" of the Social Security system.

But the results of this overhaul were more incremental tinkering with its programs, rather than an effort to refashion its structural base. The Greenspan Commission adopted 18 major recommendations that were finally approved by Congress.[17] At least five of these changes to Social Security, such as shifting COLAs, eliminating "windfall benefits," and reimbursing the Trust Funds with general revenue funds for benefits paid to the military, proposed new revenue but amounted to little more than incremental program adjustments, similar to what had been done in previous years. At least four of the changes provided benefit increases for women, to make their benefits similar to men's. Benefits were renamed as "income" for tax purposes, essentially taxing benefits for the first time. The Social Security structure based on wage-related employment and the fallacy of saving for one's own retirement were left standing without serious consideration of their continued shrinking capacity to underwrite this massive program.[18]

Conclusion: Social Security took its original authority from a set of premises that no longer support the program, while program changes that have been added have stretched the program beyond its original objectives. While these changes have been undertaken to keep Social Security relevant to current social insurance challenges, they failed to alter its original principles that established its original stable base. Instead of a coherent framework that shields its programs, Social Security today reveals paradoxes that weaken its defensibility. It was designed to provide retirement benefits based on earnings, but it also began to provide higher postretirement benefits to low-income earners. It was designed as an actuarially sound system, but reserve funds have been kept at a minimum to prevent large buildups of its assets, threatening long-term financial sustainability. Social Security was designed to preserve secure financing with a dedicated payroll tax, but the payroll tax has been frequently suspended and reduced, exposing its burden on low-income earners. Social Security was designed for aged retirees, but spouses, children, widows, widowers, and the disabled account for almost 35 percent of today's Social Security's beneficiaries. An enduring social insurance program will require a new set of supporting principles and legislative changes to establish them.

Unemployment Insurance

Unemployment Insurance, too, was part of the original Social Security Act, and like Social Security, it has outlived its original design. Unemployment Insurance was built on a set of principles that were dubious at the time, and they have become less able to sustain the programs as they have been changed over the last 80 years. Originally there was a subtle agreement that employers had some responsibility for their workers, including their unemployment, but not for job loss at another business or because of macroeconomic events.[19] It was understood as temporary, short-term financial relief until a person could get back to work. Thus, Unemployment Insurance intermingled its income protection principles of social insurances under the Social Security Act, while emphasizing putting people back to work. This comingling was intensified when the administrative responsibility for Unemployment Insurance was transferred to the Department of Labor in 1949 on the recommendation of the Hoover Commission. President Truman advocated strongly for this transfer in order to bring Unemployment Insurance into closer harmony with expectations of the Employment Act of 1946.[20]

Funding Unemployment Insurance also differed from funding Social Security. Since it was assumed that the employer should bear the burden of unemployment, a tax was levied only on the employer, even though the Treasury secretary, Henry Morgenthau, wanted the program to include a worker contribution.[21] The tax varied depending on the amount of unemployment each employer experienced, in keeping with the Wisconsin model—now called "experience rating." Taxes were collected on individual employers by the federal government and deposited into separate federal trust fund accounts designated for each state. States would then draw on these state-designated funds to pay unemployment claims, according to the eligibility conditions each set. The unemployment taxes collected from employers were used to offset excise taxes employers owed to the federal government, an early form of tax credits. In reality, therefore, the burden for financing Unemployment Insurance was borne by the federal government, not the employer. Unemployment Insurance taxes were collected under the authority of Title IX of the Social Security Act, and the Bureau of Unemployment Compensation (BUC) of the Social Security Board administered the program of Unemployment Insurance under Title III of the Social Security Act.

Employers in each state were, and still are, required to pay a fixed percent federal unemployment tax on a state-determined amount of total averaged wages—the taxable wage base (see Table 3.1). These revenues formed the basis for each state's Unemployment Insurance Trust Fund. Each state must have a trust fund large enough to pay a state-determined weekly benefit amount for at least 13 weeks of unemployment and one-half the cost of extended benefits when they are needed.

In 1970, Congress created the Extended Benefits Program, the first political recognition of the inadequacy of existing unemployment insurance; it allowed an employment benefit extension for an additional 13 weeks when unemployment in the state reached a percentage of official unemployment, usually 6 percent. Funding for the Extended Benefits Program comes from both the federal government and the state's Trust Fund. Congress also has approved temporary emergency unemployment benefits from time to time when unemployment remains high and unemployed workers are exhausting their basic benefits and their extended benefits. These temporary emergency unemployment benefits must be created anew each time Congress decides that both the basic Unemployment Insurance program and extended benefits are inadequate during times of high unemployment. When extended benefits expire, they have to be recreated by Congress. Temporary emergency unemployment benefits are fully funded by the federal government.

Table 3.1 Estimated employer contribution rates, calendar year 2013

State	Taxable Wage Base ($)	Percentage of	
		Taxable Wages	Total Wages
United States		3.22	0.86
Alabama	8,000	2.86	0.65
Alaska	36,900	2.64	1.62
Arizona	7,000	2.35	0.47
Arkansas	12,000	3.30	1.16
California	7,000	5.25	0.63
Colorado	11,300	2.66	0.68
Connecticut	15,000	4.62	1.13
Delaware	10,500	2.80	0.64
Dist. of Columbia	9,000	2.81	0.41
Florida	8,500	3.59	0.83
Georgia	9,500	2.63	0.42

Continued

Table 3.1 Continued

State	Taxable Wage Base ($)	Percentage of	
		Taxable Wages	Total Wages
Hawaii	39,600	3.23	2.22
Idaho	34,800	2.27	1.53
Illinois	12,900	4.54	1.19
Indiana	9,500	3.26	0.86
Iowa	26,000	2.11	1.15
Kansas	8,000	4.25	0.95
Kentucky	9,300	3.43	0.79
Louisiana	7,700	1.53	0.35
Maine	12,000	3.12	1.08
Maryland	8,500	3.94	0.68
Massachusetts	14,000	4.76	1.18
Michigan	9,500	6.85	1.56
Minnesota	29,000	2.74	1.31
Mississippi	14,000	1.54	0.64
Missouri	13,000	2.21	0.70
Montana	27,900	2.14	1.29
Nebraska	9,000	1.69	0.43
Nevada	26,900	2.21	1.26
New Hampshire	14,000	3.33	0.81
New Jersey	30,900	3.25	1.45
New Mexico	22,900	1.65	0.85
New York	8,500	4.54	0.67
North Carolina	20,900	1.89	0.84
North Dakota	31,800	1.12	0.68
Ohio	9,000	2.87	0.64
Oklahoma	20,100	2.49	1.13
Oregon	34,100	3.08	1.84
Pennsylvania	8,500	6.80	1.33
Puerto Rico	7,000	3.33	1.02
Rhode Island	20,200	3.88	1.63
South Carolina	12,000	2.72	0.86
South Dakota	13,000	1.07	0.38
Tennessee	9,000	3.29	0.82
Texas	9,000	2.91	0.61
Utah	30,300	1.62	0.92
Vermont	16,000	4.18	1.44
Virgin Islands	23,600	0.23	0.13
Virginia	8,000	2.33	0.44
Washington	39,800	1.84	1.06
West Virginia	12,000	3.08	1.05
Wisconsin	14,000	4.01	1.30
Wyoming	23,800	3.09	1.50

Source: US Department of Labor Employment and Training Administration.

Beneficiaries and benefits: Unemployment Insurance reflects the program's narrow focus, which is designed to get people back to work rather than assuring adequate cash support while they are not working. The beneficiary pool has been limited to people who worked in jobs specifically required to provide unemployment benefits—known as "covered employment"—which eliminated some jobs from coverage. Farm workers and textile workers, in particular were exempted from the original program, as were some small businesses. Workers are not covered if job loss is their fault, and benefit recipients are required actively look for work. Moreover, eligibility depended on working in covered employment for a specified period of time, and in later years, workers had to have also earned a certain amount of income to be eligible. For example, part-time workers are excluded from receiving unemployment benefits. Finally, the specific eligibility criteria and benefit levels were left to the states to decide. Unemployment Insurance was always considered a response to temporary unemployment. Most of the initial programs only provided benefits for a maximum of 26 weeks.

Because not all the unemployed receive Unemployment Insurance, they may not even be counted as unemployed, because they have not worked in covered employment. Only 82 percent of the civilian labor force works in covered employment, and only 61 percent of the officially unemployed received unemployment benefits in 2012. Since Unemployment Insurance benefits are time limited, 52 percent of the beneficiaries had exhausted their benefits in 2012 and were thus also lost in the unemployment count. The average weekly benefit for the United States in 2013 was $310, replacing only 47 percent of the average weekly wage. Average weekly benefit rates ranged from a high of $420 in Hawaii followed by $394 in New Jersey. Alabama paid the lowest average weekly benefit of $208. The national average weekly benefit would calculate to $16,120, well below the poverty rate for a three-person family. With the highest rate of wage replacement of 53 percent, Unemployment Insurance falls far short of a cash support program capable of sustaining unemployed workers above the poverty line (see Table 3.2).

Administration: Unemployment Insurance essentially was left to the states to administer. Benefit levels were set by each state at a level of less than 100 percent of the average weekly wage in that state, again reflecting the labor force bias in the program. Low-wage states insisted that any uniform benefit amount or eligibility criteria, beyond the most general noted above would result in labor migration. Thus an unemployed worker

Table 3.2 Average weekly UI benefits, maximum weekly UI benefits, and average UI replacement rate

State	Avg. Weekly Benefit 2013 ($)	Max Weekly Benefit 2013 ($)	Replace-ment rate from 2012 (%)	State	Avg. Weekly Benefit 2013 ($)	Max Weekly Benefit 2013 ($)	Replace-ment rate from 2012 (%)
Alabama	208	265	41	Nevada	314	402	47
Arizona	220	240	41	New	300	427	42
Arkansas	292	451	51	New Jersey	394	624	53
California	305	450	46	New Mexico	306	407	50
Colorado	366	466	50	New York	308	405	43
Connecticut	342	591	43	North	283	535	51
Delaware	251	330	42	North Dakota	414	516	48
District of	301	359	41	Ohio	318	413	46
Florida	232	275	43	Oklahoma	296	386	49
Georgia	269	330	47	Oregon	329	524	46
Hawaii	420	534	53	Pennsylvania	357	573	54
Idaho	266	357	47	Puerto Rico	118	133	37
Illinois	320	413	38	Rhode Island	354	566	56
Indiana	242	390	52	South	253	326	48
Iowa	336	396	52	South Dakota	270	333	47
Kansas	339	456	53	Tennessee	241	275	40
Kentucky	292	415	49	Texas	344	440	51
Louisiana	207	247	40	Utah	350	479	50
Maine	289	372	51	Vermont	316	425	49
Maryland	331	430	48	Virgin Islands	309	491	N/A
Massachusetts	490	674	49	Virginia	303	378	44
Michigan	293	362	49	Washington	401	604	49
Minnesota	383	393	48	West Virginia	276	424	42
Mississippi	193	235	43	Wisconsin	272	363	47
Missouri	242	320	41	Wyoming	379	459	51
Montana	294	446	46				
Nebraska	282	362	48	United States	310	412	47

Source: *The Economic Benefits of Extending Unemployment Insurance.* Washington, DC: Council of Economic Advisers and the Department of Labor, December 2013.

in Alabama would receive the Alabama unemployment benefit even if the beneficiary moved to a high wage state. The fact that today every state has a different Unemployment Insurance program is a result of a limited view of unemployment. Unemployment is an economic structural problem, and insurance, properly understood, should protect the unemployed worker with above-poverty-level benefits.

The original idea of allowing states to administer their own programs ran into trouble almost immediately. The initial plan was to require states to raise enough money to secure a state Unemployment Trust fund sufficient to provide unemployment benefits for the initial weeks of unemployment. But allowing states to set their own Taxable Wage Base, on which the 6.5 percent unemployment tax was levied, often produced trust fund shortfalls. The federal government offers states loans, which states have been quite willing to accept, hoping that as unemployment decreased, either as a result of an improved economy or as a process of unemployment attrition, they could bring their trust funds into balance without raising the taxable wage base. During spells of high unemployment, such as that experienced in the Great Recession particularly, when extended benefits were necessary, states were forced to balance their accounts and pay back the loans with interest. Thus in the present economic crisis, states simply cut back the number of initial weeks of coverage and adjusted their beneficiary formulas in order to reduce benefits paid to the unemployed thus reducing their trust fund shortages. Obviously, both the income maintenance value of unemployment insurance and its countercyclical effects were shortchanged by such state decisions.

Summary: This brief description of the program as it was created and as it has been forced to operate suggests that Unemployment Insurance was developed on a faulty structure to begin with. Unlike Social Security, which was built on a firm structure that no longer supports the burden of programs that have been added to it, the foundation for Unemployment Insurance was inadequate to supply cash support for the unemployed from the beginning. The Wisconsin model that led to experience rating, the initial inadequate tax base that left the burden on the federal government, the contradiction of program goals between income maintenance and putting people back to work, and the authority given to states to set the taxable wage rates and benefit payments, all contributed to a program that never worked very well at the beginning and has shown its inadequacy over the years, particularly during the recent Great Recession.

The United States Department of Labor grew out of the Bureau of Labor, created and placed in the Department of Interior in 1884. In the intervening years, various organized labor groups petitioned Congress repeatedly to give them a stronger voice, which it did in 1913. Lacking other administrative agencies that might be home to the developing efforts to confront poverty in the early years of the twentieth century the Labor Department housed the Children's Bureau (see Chapter 2), and was the central administrative agency in the creation of the Social Security act itself. Francis Perkins, the first woman to hold a cabinet level appointment, was chosen by President Roosevelt as his Secretary of Labor, and it was Perkins and her hand-selected staff that Roosevelt designated to develop his Economic Security Act.

The Department of Labor strongly promoted the interests of labor in the post-Depression years. It was the incubator for the rights of workers to organize and bargain with management, later realized in the Wagner Act (1935), and minimum wage and labor laws, eventually realized in the Fair Labor Standards Act (1938). By the time Unemployment Insurance was transferred to the Department of Labor in 1949, it had become much more focused on labor/management problems and labor force development. It became a controversial player in President Johnson's Great Society initiatives (see Chapter 4), and administering Unemployment Insurance became a smaller responsibility in its mission. Today the Department of Labor houses 21 Administrations, including the Employment and training administration, under which the Office of Unemployment Insurance is located. Given the administrative authority presently enjoyed by the states, it is highly unlikely that the Department of Labor would spearhead efforts to transform Unemployment Insurance into a more worker-friendly effective cash support program that could provide an effective poverty-reducing activity.

America's two most ambitious cash assistance programs were designed as social insurance programs with benefits closely tied to work. Social Security guaranteed retirement payments based on a work history during which time the worker and the employer were taxed based on worker earnings. These special tax revenues formed the basis for the amount of benefit payment guaranteed to the worker. Unemployment Insurance required employers to pay taxes (that were subsequently offset) to a state administered fund that paid benefits for currently employed workers who became unemployed through no fault of their own. States were given latitude to decide how much employers would be taxed, the conditions under which the unemployed would receive benefits, and the amount of benefit an unemployed worker would receive, within a broad framework set by the federal legislation.

Social Security expanded the beneficiary pool well beyond its original base and consistently enriched the benefits, while at the same time deliberately limiting the size of the resources needed to pay for these commitments. Its frequent financial crises provide sufficient evidence that

Social Security developed well beyond the initial structural foundation necessary to support it. While its financial problems are the most visible evidence of its structural inadequacy, the subtle drift toward a social insurance program released from strict ties to work, reflected in its broadening beneficiary pool and its growing redistributive elements, reveal a program no longer congruent with its original structural base. In short, Social Security rests on uncertain policy suppositions.

Unemployment Insurance suffers from a foundation never capable of supporting its income maintenance objectives. Always conflicted by pressure to put the unemployed back to work, and burdened by constantly changing state program administration, Unemployment Insurance was impaired by its structural foundation from the beginning. The development of Unemployment Insurance over the years only affirms its inability to meet either of its foundation objectives: income support and transitioning the unemployed back to work. The federal government has been forced frequently to intervene, first with Extended Benefits in 1970 and then with Emergency Benefits from time to time when the initial programs were incapable of keeping up with unemployment cycles. Whether the work requirements of Unemployment Insurance ever were effective, particularly in times of massive unemployment such as the recent Great Recession, the fact that Congress has been forced to provide special compensation and training to workers displaced by globalization is evidence of the inability of Unemployment Insurance to get people back to work. Outsourcing, which limits domestic work opportunities, exposes structural flaws in our economic system, and an adequate program of unemployment insurance moderates the personal impact of this latest economic development

CONSTITUTIONAL AUTHORITY FOR THE SOCIAL INSURANCES

The Constitutionality of both Social Security (Title II of the Social Security Act) and Unemployment Insurance (Title III) were secured in 1937 with *Steward Machine Co. v. Davis* by which the Court upheld the Constitutionality of the taxing power of Title IX of the Social Security Act for the purpose of funding and administering Unemployment Insurance.[22] In *Helvering v. Davis*, citing its opinion in *Steward Machine*, the Court held that Title VIII of the Social Security Act, which levied a tax on employees and employers for the use of Social Security, was therefore constitutional as well. But the Court left the final decisions about welfare to the Congress, concluding that "the line still must be drawn between one welfare and another, between general and particular."

> Where this [line] shall be placed cannot be known in advance of the event. There is a middle ground or certainly a penumbra in which discretion is large. This discretion, however, is not confined to the courts. The discretion belongs to Congress, unless the choice is clearly wrong, a display of arbitrary power, not an excess of judgment.[23]

Thus while the Court left Congress to be the final arbitrator of the general welfare power granted to it under Article I, Section 8 of the Constitution, in 1937, the income maintenance stability of both of the insurance programs has been weakened. In 1960, with the Court's decision in *Flemming v. Nestor*.[24] Flemming makes clear that (1) Social Security benefits are not a property right;[25] (2) the taxing authority of Social Security is separate from the determination and allocation of benefits;[26] and (3) Congress retains the authority to make modifications to Social Security to protect program integrity, as long as the changes are not unreasonable.[27] According to Karen Tani, *Flemming v. Nestor* was the reference for the court's decision to reduce Social Security benefits for people receiving state workmen's compensation (Unemployment Insurance) in *Richardson v. Belcher* (404 U.S. 78 [1971]). Justice Rehnquist used *Flemming v. Nestor* in *Weinberger v. Salfi* (422 U.S. 749) in 1975 as the standard for affirming the validity of Congress' authority in setting Social Security classification for beneficiaries.[28] Thus the constitutionality of Social Security is quite solid, but there are program nuances that Congress has the responsibility to address.

The Constitutional base for the social insurance programs as they have evolved make it clear that there is no beneficiary right to the programs, but rather that Congress has the Constitutional authority to create these programs and to determine their beneficiaries, thus superseding the original understanding of the authority of the insurance programs when they were created. In other words congress has the authority to change the scope of both programs in order to match the demands of twenty-first-century social insurance obligations.

The work conundrum: By this time it should be evident that resting social insurance programs under the shelter of work has severe limitations in America's twenty-first-century social welfare enterprise. The changes in the labor market discussed in Chapters 2 and 5 should provide ample justification to conclude that limiting social insurance participation and benefits by workforce attachment no longer suffices as a foundation for either Social Security or Unemployment Insurance. Social Security has already shifted toward a new social insurance framework more consistent with twenty-first-century America, and with this shift it is difficult to envision that Social Security's antiquated method of financing, the payroll tax, can withstand further demands as Social Security continues its present trajectory. Limiting benefits, either by across-the-board reductions or selective program modifications, simply pushes serious financing problems into the future or continues to place a major welfare burden on a dwindling work force. Such incremental changes only forestall the development of a social welfare system capable of reducing poverty.

CONCLUSION

The Social Insurances are too important for Americans and the American economy to fail for lack of financing, and they are essential as cash support for poor people. They keep some Americans out of poverty and provide important financial resources for those who continue to remain poor. Both Social Security and Unemployment Insurance have expanded well beyond their basic intentions, and Social Security in particular has considerable capacity for reducing poverty and its consequences on the poor. Most organizations committed to protecting Social Security, like AARP, would do so by raising payroll taxes. There is also considerable support for removing the earnings cap, which today stands at $113,700, after which no Social Security taxes are paid. But tinkering with the payroll tax avoids the fundamental problems of the payroll tax discussed above, and it continues the macroeconomic arguments that led to keeping the taxes low in the first place. Today's payroll tax of 12.4 percent, half paid by the employer, constitutes a heavy tax burden on worker earnings rather than income. As Social Security continues to morph into a pay-as-you-go retirement system, whereby today's taxes pay today's benefits, the payroll tax loses its political value as a contribution to one's own future retirement. In other words any distinction between the payroll tax and general revenue taxes gradually has been lost over the years and the economic protection the trust fund provides to Social Security is arguable particularly in times high unemployment and low-paying employment. The payroll tax fails to produce protection or parity for Social Security.[29]

Unemployment Insurance has demonstrated its weaknesses over the years and certainly during the Great Recession. Its income maintenance benefits are limited by time worked and by level of support. The taxing structure for Unemployment Insurance rests the financial burden of the program on the federal government, while the fundamental decisions of eligibility for benefits and benefit amount rests with the states. Perhaps more than any other social welfare program, Unemployment Insurance has revealed its income maintenance inadequacy during the Great Recession, which clearly exposed America's structural weaknesses to provide benefits for its citizens. The structural reforms needed for the social insurances are discussed in Chapter 7; relocating these reforms on a secure foundation has become necessary for the individuals who depend on them, for their capacity to lift people out of poverty, and for the continued successful development of American capitalism.

BOX 3.2   GREENSPAN COMMISSION RECOMMENDATIONS*

Increase tax rate on covered wages and salaries

Increase tax rate on covered self-employment earnings

Cover all federal elected officials and political appointees

Cover new federal employees

Cover all nonprofit employees

Prohibit State and local government terminations

Accelerate collection of State and local taxes

Modify general fund reimbursement methods for military service credits

Provide general fund transfers for unnegotiated checks

Delay benefit increases 6 months

Limit benefit increases to lesser of wage or price increase, under certain conditions Continue benefits on remarriage

Modify indexing of deferred survivor benefits

Raise disabled widow(er)'s benefits to 71.5 percent of PIA

Pay divorced spouses whether or not worker has retired

Replace 90-percent factor in benefit formula with variable percentage, for individuals receiving pensions from non-covered employment

Offset spouses' benefits by up to two-thirds of non-covered government pension

Expand use of death certificates to stop benefits

Impose 5-year residency requirement for certain aliens

Tax one-half of benefits for high-income beneficiaries

Source: John A. Svahn and Mary Ross, Social Security Amendments of 1983: Legislative History and Summary of Provisions. *Social Security Bulletin*, July 1983/Vol. 46, No. 7.

4. Cash Support Assistance Programs ❧

The cash support assistance programs constitute a second type of cash support identified in the Introduction and discussed briefly in Chapter 1. There are two such programs administered under the Social Security Act: Supplemental Security Income (SSI) and Temporary Assistance to Needy Families (TANF) (see Figure I.1). Chapter 3 notes that the social insurances were established on the principle that people who have worked build up work-related benefits that are available to them when they are unable to work, due to age or disability (Social Security) or through loss of jobs (unemployment insurance). The cash support assistance programs, however, are based on an economic indulgence to the financially needy aged and disabled (SSI) and children (TANF). The two program types—cash support social insurance and cash support assistance—were designed for different purposes, but as time has gone on, they have overlapped one another. For example, if a person benefits from a social insurance program, but still has economic need, the person may receive cash assistance. This kind of cash support assistance is often called "welfare" because it is based on the income need of the individual; it is America's most contestable social welfare undertaking.

The reason for the separation of cash support into two categories—those who have worked and those who have economic need whether they have worked or not—is discussed briefly in Chapters 2 and 3, but the history of America's response to poverty discussed in Chapter 1 affirms a disdain for the poor and the parsimonious use of cash to elevate their economic circumstances. However, Chapter 2 argues that economic need may be a result of economic forces outside an individual's capacity to change, as the Great Depression and the Great Recession demonstrate. Sorting economic need driven by personal behavior from that produced by features of American capitalism has produced sterile arguments that differentiate the "worthy," namely those who work or have worked, from those "unworthy" poor, those who have not worked or have not worked enough. Too often that distinction burdens the provision of cash support with ideological partialities, forcing the poor to behave in prescribed ways that are not expected of those who are not poor. While no one can claim a right to programs designed to satisfy economic need, neither can these programs abuse the rights of those who receive them.[1] Deliberately or otherwise, while constitutional freedoms are not abridged by such practices, full freedom of expression may be lost by those forced to depend on welfare programs.[2]

Certainly the American political system has acquiesced to American capitalism when economic events have collided with preferred neoclassical economic features, as the Great Recession clearly demonstrated. Government fiscal relief was available to financial institutions, but fiscal relief to individuals through the social welfare enterprise was halting and inadequate to the task of preventing severe individual economic losses. The political reluctance to adjust cash support assistance programs to accommodate those in economic need during times of structural economic failure reflects beliefs that programs that shore up people in economic need burden America's neoclassical economic system rather than promote opportunities for economic and social development as might be inferred from Keynesian economics. For example, during the Great Recession, some economists and many politicians were calling for *reductions* in cash support assistance programs as a way to strengthen the economy, and unemployment insurance was a frequent victim of this historic misunderstanding of America's social welfare necessity.

The separation of social insurance cash support from assistance cash support fit a neoclassical economic model that argued that there should be no unemployment in a well-functioning economic system, implying that poverty is an individual failure, not a structural one. As was discussed in Chapter 3, changes in America's economic structure, however, have bent the social insurances away from strictly work-related benefits. In the same way, changes in the American economy have produced work that does not eliminate economic need, increasing the pressure for cash assistance for those who cannot work or whose work is not economically sufficient for their basic needs. Yet a distinction between structural and personal economic poverty continues to define the difference between social welfare as social insurance and social welfare as cash assistance. The Great Recession exposed the fallacy of this distinction as the cash assistance programs proved inadequate protection against economic loss and poverty.

THE CASH SUPPORT ASSISTANCE PROGRAMS

Today, Supplemental Security (SSI) and Temporary Assistance to Needy Families (TANF) have been distilled from four previous programs administered under the Social Security Act designed to provide financial assistance to four categories of economically needy people: the aged, blind, disabled, and children. The aged, blind, and disabled have been lumped into SSI, and children receive cash assistance through TANF. Both the early cash assistance programs and their present-day generation lack a lucid basis for their existence and a coherent purpose for their future development. Their inclusion in the Social Security Act confirmed the need for federal funding and perpetuated the beliefs that these programs constituted a last resort to assist poor people. In other words, the assistance programs were not part of the grand design for Social Security. In fact the assistance programs threatened the development of the social insurances, which anticipated a social welfare system that "paid benefits as a matter of right through the Social Security system and that used the public assistance system as a means of aiding families and making them function at home and in the labor force."[3] In 1945, the American Public Welfare Association (APWA) formally stated, "The need for public assistance [should] be reduced to a minimum through strengthening the social insurance programs with respect to coverage and adequacy of benefit payments."[4] APWA advocated for social rehabilitation for those still left out of the social insurance fold, an issue discussed below.

In spite of the new role the federal government assumed with the Social Security Act, the structural foundation for the assistance programs remained fixed in the historic framework of social welfare discussed in Chapter 2. While the social insurances recognized the need for social welfare provoked by the rising unemployment occasioned by the Great Depression, the cash assistance programs remained cemented in individual explanations for their necessity. The historic solution to economic dependency had integrated a frugal provision of cash with established formal efforts to "rehabilitate" the poor, sometimes with punitive sanctions and sometimes with "helpful" services, such as marriage counseling to preserve two-parent families. Thus, a strategy consisting of social services for those who needed financial assistance contrasted with the income strategy of the social insurances and infused the development of the assistance programs with different economic and political destinies. While the economics and politics of the social insurances struggled with financing and expanding the beneficiary pool, the economics and politics of a service strategy struggled with balancing the need for cash assistance with various debates over the kinds of services that would lift people out of poverty. For the most part, economists prevailed in the politics of social insurance, but there was, at best, confusing social welfare authority to guide the political debates over helping people out of poverty. Aside from the conventional wisdom that the poor should not be made too comfortable with any financial assistance, the kinds of services that would help them escape poverty were driven by constantly changing socially fashionable ideas based on available research of the day. Thus, not only were cash assistance payments held low, but those who received them were subject to constantly changing pressures to behave in ways presumed to overcome their poverty.

Social Security administrators struggled with the inherent conflict between efforts to expand the social insurances and the continued need for funding the cash assistance programs, as it became more evident that the former would not significantly alter the latter. As noted in the previous chapter, improving the beneficiary payments and expanding the beneficiary pool helped reduce those elderly receiving cash assistance, but the more fundamental problem

> stemmed from a difference in program structure that seemed less important when OASI [Social Security] benefit levels and coverage were more modest and when [cash assistance] and OASI dealt with essentially distinct populations that overlapped only minimally. As Congress repeatedly increased OASI benefits from 1950 through 1973, it occasionally adjusted the terms for federal contribution to state [cash assistance] programs to induce or permit similar increases, but [leaving] each state final authority over its OAA [Old Age Assistance] benefit levels.[5]

Trying to integrate the work-based social insurance with economic need led to calls for some sort of standard program of guaranteed cash income for the latter lest the former be forced out of its work-related benefit structure. On the other hand, if cash assistance were to remain tethered to social insurance principles, then those in financial need had to be helped to get work and build up work-related insurance benefits. Either consideration called for social rehabilitation and led to calls for the traditional service strategy as a way to reduce poverty.

SUPPLEMENTAL SECURITY INCOME

Supplemental Security Income (SSI) represents a compelling example of social welfare wandering through economic and political encounters without a sufficient foundation to guide its development. The SSI story begins with the original Social Security Act in 1935 when the social insurances and the financial assistance programs were created. Deliberately left to the states to administer, Old Age Assistance, Aid for the Blind, and Aid for Dependent Children provided need-based cash assistance to people in these three groups who met state-determined eligibility criteria. But while the states administered these programs, most of the funding for them came from the federal government through the use of a grant-in-aid that tied federal money to a proportional amount that states were required to put into these programs. The federal government used its financial support to states to juggle insurance/assistance issues, while the states had their own perspective on need-based cash assistance. The resulting grant-in-aid approach to funding cash assistance produced a history of acrimony between the states and the federal government over who would set the standard for the amount of aid provided and under what conditions it would be given. This financing approach to cash assistance left the basic structure of need-based cash assistance programs with the states, which the Committee on Economic Security intended, but constantly pressured states to do things they were often unwilling to do.

The creation of Supplemental Security Income (SSI) in 1972 represented a major shift in America's cash support commitments, all of which were under the authority of the Social Security Act at that time, except for the Food Stamp Program. A sequence of economic, political, and social bickering about poverty and cash support came together in a chain of events that not only shifted the responsibility for the nation's welfare programs to the federal government, but also laid the foundation for the Earned Income Tax Credit (EITC) discussed in the next chapter. The subsequent inability of SSI to have a positive impact on poverty provides further evidence that America's cash support commitments lack sufficient political or economic will to support them and have no clear social welfare foundation to direct them.

ECONOMIC DEBATES

The idea of putting all the cash assistance (welfare) programs together by eliminating categories of cash assistance recipients emerged from time to time and was usually stymied by lack of agreement over who would administer them, and, most importantly, who would pay for them.[6] The failed War on Poverty, however, left one continuing legacy for the assistance programs: an income strategy, not a service strategy emerged as the best way to address economic need. The idea of a Guaranteed Annual Income (GAI), or some form of income guarantee to replace the categorical cash assistance programs materialized from economists as a way to both stabilize existing welfare programs and to eliminate the War on Poverty's discredited service strategy. As early as 1962, Milton Friedman, the neoconservative economist at the University of Chicago, proposed a cash income guarantee to the poor as an approach that would provide them with needed income while lowering the profile of government in its efforts to manage the economy.[7] For Friedman and conservative economists, a government guaranteed annual income would also be more efficient than the existing system of state-administered cash assistance programs with their cumbersome social services. Liberal economists, too, liked the idea because it represented an application of Keynesian economics to the socioeconomic system, which "by default, still left [it] to the working of the 'invisible hand'."[8]

In 1968, some of the leading economists meeting in Cambridge, Massachusetts petitioned Congress to develop a GAI as a means to consolidate the existing cash assistance programs.[9] President Johnson established a Commission on Income Maintenance in 1968 that recommended "the creation of a universal income supplement program financed and administered by the Federal Government making cash payments to all members of the population with income need."[10] These recommendations never got to Congress in a legislative form.[11]

POLITICAL WANDERINGS

Supplemental Security Income developed in a vastly changed political environment from that which supported President Johnson's Great Society undertakings. President Nixon's election not only signaled a national partisan political realignment, but the Nixon presidency also brought a changed breed of people into federal social welfare administration: advocates of the newly developing administrative practice known as Program Planning and Budgeting Systems (PPBS)—presumably a method for streamlining government. His appointment of Casper Weinberger, known as "Cap the Knife" as secretary of the Department of Health, Education and Welfare signaled Nixon's eagerness to dismantle as much of the Kennedy-Johnson service-oriented social welfare architecture as he could by replacing most career executives in the Department of Health, Education and Welfare with "Level C" management oriented executives.[12] Results-oriented administrators who had not been groomed by the social welfare establishment replaced seasoned social welfare administrators. Weinberger was particularly critical of social services that seemed to have no effect on reducing welfare dependency.[13] Wilbur Cohen, a strong advocate and highly respected social welfare elder who had been in the department since its inception, was named secretary by President Johnson in 1968, but Nixon replaced him with Elliott Richardson, who quickly was replaced by Weinberger.

The Moynihan enigma: Yet the most transforming political event in the development of SSI arguably was wrapped up in the perplexing political career of Patrick David Moynihan. Hired by Secretary of Labor Arthur Goldberg as an assistant secretary for policy, Moynihan was closely involved in the development of the War on Poverty. Based on his own research, Moynihan authored a controversial report on "the Negro family in America," arguing that the breakdown of the Negro family structure was a major cause of African American poverty. When President Johnson used a good part of this report in a speech at Howard University, a major controversy erupted. The furor contributed to the growing strain on Moynihan's relationship with the president, which had originated with Moynihan's public support of Robert Kennedy's political ambitions. Disillusioned by the War on Poverty and President Johnson's coldness, Moynihan sent the newly elected President Nixon a letter outlining his views on welfare reform. Nixon, like most of his predecessors and successors who wanted to reform welfare, was intrigued by Moynihan's proposals. Nixon invited Moynihan to chair his newly created Urban Affairs Council, and charged it with developing his welfare reform agenda.

Moynihan's public contempt for single-parent families—usually referred to as "broken homes"—as stated in his now infamous *Moynihan Report*,[14] his familiarity with proposals for a guaranteed income, and his disdain for social services as provided by the War on Poverty, grounded his welfare reform design. His own childhood undoubtedly conditioned him to the problems of growing up in a single-parent household and to dismiss social workers. Thus, Moynihan fashioned Nixon's welfare reform as a novel Family Assistance Plan (FAP) that proposed to strengthen families[15] and reduce poverty through a negative income tax that had already been proposed to Nixon by the Department of the Treasury. Devoid of any social services, the guaranteed income appealed to Moynihan when he served as director of the Joint Center for Urban Studies, Massachusetts

Institute of Technology and Harvard University during the debates over the use of a guaranteed annual income.

Nixon's FAP was never popular with Congress. The first version introduced in 1969 passed the House of Representatives, but after three days of hearings, the Senate requested that the administration withdraw the bill, which it did. It then introduced a significantly altered version of FAP in 1970, but the Senate claimed it did not modify its stringent work requirements, raise the low level of the income guarantee, or protect the social service commitments established during the Kennedy-Johnson years. The Senate held hearings on FAP throughout the 91st Congress until it adjourned. President Nixon introduced yet another version of FAP in 1971 as soon as the new Congress convened. This one went through a torturous Congressional process, generating six volumes of Senate Finance Committee transcripts and a 1,285-page report. By the time Congress was finished with it, FAP emerged in 1972 without a negative income tax and a minimal guaranteed income that was no better than what most states were providing under their existing cash assistance programs. Perhaps most significantly, SSI was no longer a *Family* Assistance Plan: Congress declined to include the Aid for Families with Dependent Children (AFDC) program into SSI, leaving it standing as the last grant-in-aid cash assistance program created under the original Social Security Act, and a candidate for further welfare reform.

Fashionable families: The years leading up to Moynihan's welfare reform proposal were marked by increased attention to the American family by Congress, as noted in Chapter 1. The poverty literature continually linked female-headed families with greater poverty, a point strongly made in Moynihan's report. The Social Security' Act's original cash assistance program, Aid for Dependent Children (ADC, Title IV of the original Social Security Act) was frequently blamed for aggravating poverty. Since the cash support was provided to a financially dependent child due to the financial absence of an adult caretaker, critics argued that ADC encouraged fathers to desert their families so their children would be eligible for cash assistance. It was a spurious argument, at best, yet ADC changed its focus and name to Aid to *Families* with Dependent Children (AFDC) in 1959, including unemployed parents in a family cash assistance grant. The grant was to aid the family in the belief that two-parent families lowered poverty among children, while single-parent families contributed to it.[16] Thus began the shift to family-centered social welfare, exposing the problem that a family was not easily defined by its particular structure. And as AFDC caseloads began to rise significantly, the program came under further attack as an actual cause of financial dependency since a female-headed household was now considered a family, and it could still receive cash assistance whether a father remained in the home or was absent from it. Moynihan's FAP reform stated: "The present AFDC system encourages dependency. The preferential treatment of female-headed families has led to increased family breakup. In 1940, 30 percent of AFDC families had absent fathers; today it is over 70 percent."[17]

Underlying policy issues for SSI: The details of Congress' objections to Nixon's Family Assistance Plan, which transformed it from an income guarantee to a diluted system of cash support, explain in large part the subsequent development of the EITC and Temporary Assistance to Needy Families (TANF). When isolated from the political acrimony between Nixon and Congress, the substance of the dispute over Nixon's welfare reform (known as HR 1) centered on a family-based welfare program, as contrasted with an individual-based welfare program, and a subtle shift to family responsibility for the child's economic situation. While this modification of financial responsibility represented a liberalization of financial aid for dependent children, by bringing both of their parents under the cash assistance program, it carried with it a delicate transition in the nation's responsibility for the welfare of children. Whereas historically children were the unit of cash assistance, now the family became the beneficiary.

SSI avoided the growing controversies over the financial dependency of an individual or a family by sticking with the historical categorical approach to cash assistance: assistance to the aged and disabled (SSI considered the blind disabled and not a separate assistance category). Since children were now viewed a part of a family, regardless of its structure, Aid to Families with Dependent Children (AFDC) was left to stand alone. Children were included in the original SSI legislation only if they met the criteria for disability "comparable with that of an adult," which subsequently was altered in 1996 after the Supreme Court ruled the criteria was unconstitutional.[18] This inconsistency of giving financial aid to an economically dependent disabled child but denying similar aid to able-bodied financially dependent children simply continued the rancorous debates over providing financial assistance to families without requiring work in exchange for the benefit. While children were exempt from work requirements, welfare critics argued that family members were expected to work for financial benefits provided to the child, even though the head of the family was most likely a single woman whose employment potential was weak.

Finally, if adult family members were expected to work, there was disagreement over how earned income would affect benefit. SSI avoided this issue as well. This problem of reducing benefits proportionally with earnings from work could not be resolved and remained a problem later as President Carter also sought to reform welfare. Thus Congress created SSI, leaving cash assistance on behalf of children as Aid to Families with Dependent Children in place until it, too, was reformed into Temporary Assistance for Needy Families (TANF) in 1996. The SSI benefit was established on the basis of an individual's or couple's income, although in the case of a disabled child, SSI eligibility was based on family income. For Congress, children who were not disabled and who whose families received assistance constituted a different class of financially dependent children, and to date, no one has challenged this assessment.

THE PROGRAM

In 1974, SSI began paying benefits to about 4 million disabled people and aged adults. In fiscal year 2013, the program made payments to more than 8 million people at a cost to the federal government of about $53 billion, according to the Congressional Budget Office. The guidelines for SSI eligibility are set by the Social Security Administration, which administers the program in cooperation with the states. For 2014, the income thresholds for eligibility were $721 per individual or $1,082 per couple, per month. In other words, people below these income thresholds are eligible to apply for SSI. But there are asset limits as well: a maximum of $2,000 per individual and $3,000 per couple. SSI payments are usually much less than these basic income guarantees because earned income, in-kind income, deemed income, and insurance are counted against the guarantee: $65.00 per month for earned income and $20.00 per month for unearned income is disregarded when calculating financial need. Social Security is counted as unearned income, allowing a $20 per month exception, also known as a "pass-through."

Originally, states were required to make up the difference between their Aid to Aged, Aid to the Blind, and Aid to Disabled programs and the federal guarantee. Today, about half of the states continue to supplement federal payments. The numerous disregarded income pass-throughs and supplements meant that the average monthly benefit payments varied. The average payment was $526, but for the aged, it was $415, the disabled, $544, children, $627, adults, $543, and over age 65, $423 in 2013. Without

Table 4.1 Average monthly SSI payment, by eligibility category, age, and source of payment, October 2013

	Eligibility Category			Age		
	All	Aged	Blind/Disabled	Under 18	18–64	65 and over
All sources	526.35	415.26	544.27	626.87	543.62	423.23
Federal only	507.32	376.95	527.54	618.77	526.21	338.61
State supplement	121.38	130.36	118.52	48.44	129	131.27

Source: Social Security Administration, Supplemental Security Record, 100 percent data, April, 2014 (eligibility category and age are not exclusive).

state supplementation, however, the average benefit payments were much lower: the average benefit was $507, while the aged usually received $377, the disabled $528, children $619, adults $526, and for people over age 65, $389 (see Table 4.1).

Although the number of SSI beneficiaries has increased, and continues to do so, the number of aged SSI beneficiaries has decreased as Social Security benefits have continued to rise. The number of disabled children receiving SSI has increased steadily since the 1996 *Sullivan* ruling, noted above. SSI disability means one of a set of medical conditions severe enough to prevent aged and disabled recipients from participating in "substantial gainful activity," which in 2012 was considered to mean work that would produce earnings of more than $1,010 a month. The SSI program (assistance) and Social Security (social insurance) overlap in several ways. Most significantly, the Social Security benefit is counted as a resource (less $20.00) for computing the SSI benefit. Approximately 57 percent of the aged who receive SSI also receive Social Security, but as a result of SSI eligibility criteria, the value of their Social Security is reduced to $20.00 per month. This means that, in effect, the value of work, a keystone of the social insurances, is lost for this group of aged. SSI also overlaps other cash support programs: TANF, SNAP, and EITC.

The SSI income thresholds (maximum income for a SSI recipient) fail to reduce poverty. The income threshold for a single person constitutes only 73 percent of the poverty line and 83 percent of the poverty line for a couple. In 1992, a feeble effort was made to acknowledge reduction of poverty as a SSI social welfare goal and bring Supplemental Security Income into better harmony with other social welfare programs authorized by the Social Security Act, including Aid to Families with Dependent Children program (Title IV of the Social Security Act). Social Security

Commissioner Gwendolyn King, responsible for the administration of SSI, commissioned the formation of a panel of experts to study the SSI program and make recommendations for its modernization. Former secretary of HEW Arthur Flemming chaired the 21-person panel. The report stated that the "SSI program is an integral part of the nation's total social security program. Social Security is an umbrella title that was used in 1935 for ten closely related programs. The programs under Social Security are dependent one another to attempt to lift people out of poverty." The panel recommended that SSI be changed to "increase the Federal benefit standard for an individual, in 5 equal annual increments, to 120 percent of the poverty guideline." It also recommended steps to bring more children from Title IV under SSI and bring SSI into closer harmony with Social Security.[19] Nothing was done with these recommendations, and no further suggestions have been made to bring social welfare programs into better harmony with the need to reduce poverty since then, perpetuating the already unstable foundation of the cash assistance programs.

Temporary Assistance to Needy Families

From 1972 until 1996, cash assistance on behalf of children (AFDC) continued to be provided as a grant-in-aid to states, as had aid to the aged, blind and disabled before SSI was created. SSI provided a partial solution to the problem raised by the cash support of the social insurances related to work attachment, and cash assistance burdened with social services. SSI gave the cash assistance programs a service-free structural home under the umbrella of the Social Security Administration, even though the consolidation perpetuated the distinction of benefits earned by work (insurance) and benefits based on need (assistance). Nor did SSI economically lift the aged, blind, and disabled above the poverty level. Since people in these groups were not expected to work, however, merging the three cash assistance programs avoided any need for social rehabilitation to make them workforce eligible.[20] SSI also sidestepped the problem of family-centered social welfare by leaving social welfare need defined by the traditional categories of beneficiaries: aged and disabled. SSI was not a Family Assistance Plan as originally proposed. These issues remained unaddressed in the stand-alone Aid to Families with Dependent Children program until they surfaced in Newt Gingrich's "Contract with America," and from President Clinton, who vowed to completely change welfare (meaning AFDC) as we know it. Temporary Assistance to Needy Families (TANF) emerged from another testy political climate in 1996.

Welfare's war on women: According to the 1935 Social Security Act, which created the original cash assistance program, Aid to Dependent Children, a "dependent child means a child under the age of sixteen who has been deprived of parental support or care by reason of the death, continued absence from the home, or physical or mental incapacity of a parent, and who is living…in a place of residence maintained by one or more of such relatives as his or her own home."[21] Statutory reasons for "continued absence from the home" included divorce, legal and voluntary separation, desertion, imprisonment, and never marrying.

Perhaps it is simply a historical stereotype, but women, as mothers, rather than men, as fathers, have been the default child caretakers and therefore tend to receive the cash assistance provided to economically dependent children in cases where there is an absent parent. Obviously the reasons for continued absence from the home cannot be easily attributed to either a mother or a father, but the mother, not the father has always been the preferred parent to care for children. A 1961 study by the Social Security Administration found that over 80 percent of the children receiving AFDC were deprived of care or support because of the death, disability, absence, or unemployment of the *father*, not the *mother*,[22] even though the reason a supporting father was absent from the home was not directly recognized as the mother's choice, and the mother was left with the care of the child.

After the 1959 family-friendly changes noted above allowing cash support to children when fathers were living in the home, efforts mounted to socially rehabilitate families. Because there were so few fathers living in the family household, women became the default parent to receive social services designed to reduce welfare costs. Beginning in 1962, Congress provided money and legislative authority for social services designed to help families and individuals become self-supporting rather than dependent upon welfare. At first these services were voluntary and were focused on unemployed fathers living in the home with the financially dependent children, but as it became evident that there were few participating fathers, Congress created the Work Incentive Program (WIN) in 1967 as a modification to these early voluntary rehabilitation services.[23] The WIN program required all AFDC parents, mostly mothers by this time, to register for vocational training, counseling, and/or assistance in obtaining basic education and job skills. According to the First Annual WIN Report in 1970, 71 percent of the WIN population was female.

By 1971, research studies concluded that the program was not effectively enlisting welfare mothers in work, nor was it reducing welfare expenditures. So, Congress amended WIN in 1971, and again in 1980, again in 1982, and yet again in 1984, each time tightening requirements for mandatory participation in the program with greater pressures to replace welfare with work.[24] The Family Support Act of 1988 (Job Opportunities and Basic Skills, aka JOBS, P.L. 100–485) replaced WIN, and all states had to transfer to the JOBS program by October 1990. The JOBS program intensified the pressure to move mothers into work and away from welfare under AFDC by focusing on people who had received AFDC for at least 36 months. It required participation by parents of children as young as three years old and permitted states to include participation of mothers with children as young as one year old. These efforts are more remarkable in the context that it took until 1975 (P.L. 93–647) for Congress to create the Child Support Enforcement program that provided legislative recognition of the fact that fathers, indeed, had equal financial responsibility for their dependent children, whether the father lived in the home or not, by passing legislation establishing stringent conditions for identifying and finding absent fathers of financially dependent children, establishing legal paternity of their dependent children, and establishing and enforcing child financial support orders.[25] Even so, mothers still remained responsible for the care and economic support of their children, whether they received child support payments or not. Thus mothers have been subject to the pressures and indignities that have come with social rehabilitation efforts to assure that they will be financially able to care for their children.

TANF, the nuclear option: The failed Family Assistance Plan set off this series of efforts to refocus the economic needs of children within a family and to replace cash assistance to dependent children with income from their mother's work, setting the political stage for a final reform. In spite of the research documenting the failure of the stream of welfare-to-work programs[26] outlined above, another president, William J. Clinton, tried his hand at yet another. Some of the most hostile measures welfare ever inflicted on women who cared for dependent children emerged from this 1996 welfare initiative, as detailed below.

This much-discussed federal welfare reform legislation started out in the first session of the 104th Congress as part of the "Contract with America," which was set forth by the Republican majority in the House of Representatives, but was not inconsistent with President Clinton's pledge to "end welfare as we now know it." The first House of Representatives version of this bill, HR 4, was included as part of the December 1995 budget bill when it did not win full Congressional approval on its own. The president vetoed this budget bill, leading to a shutdown of the federal government for almost two weeks. The House of Representatives subsequently revised parts of HR 4 and presented a freestanding welfare reform bill to the president at the beginning of the second session of the 104th Congress in January 1996, but the president vetoed this version as well.

The president's objection to Congress' welfare reform efforts appeared more political than ideological.[27] Thus Representative E. Clay Shaw (R. Fla.), chairman of the House Ways and Means Welfare Reform subcommittee, revived the legislation as HR 3734, and led it through minor modifications, thus winning the president's approval. The president announced on July 31, 1996 that he would sign the compromise legislation. The House of Representatives approved the Conference Committee Report on July 31, and the Senate approved it August 1, 1996. The president signed the bill August 22, 1996, making welfare reform a reality.

Ron Haskins, the reputed driving force behind TANF, called work the "cannonball" of the Republican welfare reform agenda and the solution to welfare.[28] The most nefarious legacy of the 1996 welfare reform can be found in the use of public policy to control individual behavior. Lawrence Meade brought considerable intellectual energy to this significant change for providing income for poor children. Meade argued that economic aid should be provided in exchange for "good behavior" not on "impersonal" economic need.[29] Haskins states, "Other than giving money to the poor as we did with Social Security benefits for the elderly, arguably the best strategy the federal government and the states have adopted to reduce poverty is to encourage, cajole, or force poor mothers on welfare to work."[30]

TANF program structure: TANF made major changes to the Aid to Families with Dependent Children (AFDC) program. The most significant structural change turned the grant-in-aid for cash assistance to children and their families into a block grant to states. The block grant decreased federal oversight of cash assistance and provided states with flexibility in the use of federal funds. Those that were granted under TANF no longer had to be used specifically for cash grants, but could be used for "assistance" and "non-assistance" purposes. Assistance includes basic needs as well as child care and transportation assistance for those who are not employed. Non-assistance includes child care, transportation assistance and other supports for those who are employed, nonrecurring short-term benefits, Individual Development Accounts, refundable earned income tax credits, work subsidies to employers, and services such as education and training, case management, job search, and counseling."[31]

TANF beneficiary changes: In addition to the important structural changes in cash assistance to financially dependent families and children,

TANF instituted program changes that had a direct effect on beneficiaries. States must require a percentage of adult TANF recipients to work if they are not exempted because of disability or taking care of a minor child. TANF also sets a 5-year lifetime time limit on continued program eligibility.[32] A major exception applies to children when they are not living with a parent or when a parent is in the home but is ineligible for assistance; this protects the interests of children when they are not in an eligible family. In these instances, at the discretion of each state, only the children receive cash assistance. These cases constitute about half of all TANF beneficiaries.[33]

TANF outcomes: In 2009, federal and state spending for TANF was $30.6 billion. While the number of TANF cases showed a decline leading up to the Great Recession, they jumped significantly by almost 200,000 between 2008 and 2009 to approximately 1.9 million.[34] As a result of the Great Recession, the American Recovery and Reinvestment Act of 2009 had to create the TANF Emergency Contingency Fund of $5 billion to reimburse TANF administrative jurisdictions (usually the states) that had an increase in assistance caseloads in FY 2009 and FY 2010 because the program lacked the capacity to respond to this structural economic crisis. The average monthly amount of cash assistance for TANF recipient families was $389 in FY 2009, $324 for one child, $408 for two children, $496 for three children, and $592 for four or more children. About one-sixth of TANF families included at least one person also receiving SSI. Only 23 percent of TANF funds were spent on cash assistance. The remainder was spent for childcare, transportation and other supportive services (see Figure 4.1).

TANF has been credited with significantly lowering the welfare caseload, but it is clear that the work requirements have had little value in reducing welfare dependency among children. TANF caseloads have declined, but the latest TANF report concluded that only 17 percent of the closed cases in 2009 were due to employment. The average monthly income for a three-person family that left TANF due to employment was $1,018 per month, still only 63 percent of the established poverty threshold but more than TANF eligibility in most states.[35]

Authoritative evaluations of the impact of TANF on parents and their children have been sparse. The General Accounting Office (GAO) undertook a very limited study of TANF employment issues in 1999 and found that most of the adults in families remaining off the welfare rolls were employed at some time after leaving welfare, but GAO found that from 19 to 30 percent of the families who left welfare returned to the rolls at some time during a follow-up period. Many families who had left welfare

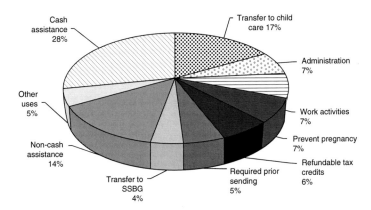

Figure 4.1 TANF spending by category
Source: TANF Ninth Annual Report to Congress, 2012.

continued to receive noncash assistance, indicating that families' incomes were low enough to keep them eligible for these other forms of government assistance. The GAO report concluded,

> The limited information on economic status of the families being tracked indicates that many families who leave welfare find jobs that are low-paying. The low wages of these jobs emphasize the importance that income supports, such as subsidized medical and child care and the earned income credit, can assume in these families' total financial resources.[36]

Using various census data, the Women's Legal Defense and Education Fund reports that in 1996, only 28 percent of poor children were *not* receiving welfare assistance under the AFDC program, but by 2012 the percentage of poor children *not* receiving TANF support had risen to 74 percent.[37] Ladonna Paveth concluded her year 2000 extensive evaluation of the TANF program by noting that "it has been implemented during extraordinary times. Low unemployment rates have made it far easier to place welfare recipients in jobs than anyone anticipated.... However, until the country experiences a recession, no one will know whether the assistance system that is being established can be sustained over the long term."[38] The Great Recession provided an answer.

TANF and social welfare tradeoffs: TANF has not eliminated the need for other social welfare benefits, and as TANF caseloads have been reduced other social programs have grown, suggesting that TANF transfers the poverty burden to other programs. Steve Wamhoff and Michael

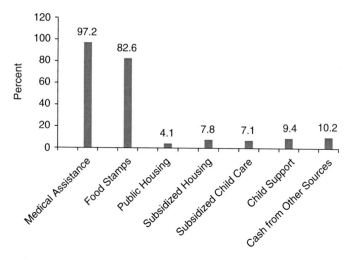

Figure 4.2   Percentage of TANF families receiving
Source: TANF Tenth Annual Report to Congress.

Wiseman report that there are also program and individual beneficiary advantages to transferring disabled adults and children to SSI. States gain because the federal government pays for the SSI benefit, and states can then use the TANF savings for other purposes. The families gain because the SSI benefits they acquire are greater than the TANF benefits they lose. The work participation requirements under TANF also require states to meet TANF's work requirements, and states can avoid these costs if adults have disabilities that satisfy SSI eligibility requirements. The incentives for TANF recipients to transfer for SSI account in large measure for the large increases in the SSI caseload, particularly as inflation has caused real TANF benefits to fall relative to payments received by SSI recipients.[39] Figure 4.2 shows the relationship between TANF financial support, SNAP and other means-tested social welfare programs.

SUMMARY

In the cause of children: America has a storied legacy of efforts to promote and protect children's interests: the "child saving" movement begun by Reverend Charles Brace as an alternative to child apprenticeship (circa 1853–1964), the New York Children's Aid Society (1853), the Society for the Prevention of Cruelty to Children (1870), the work of social reformers that led to the White House Conference on Children (1910), and the subsequent creation of the Children's Bureau (1912), accompanied by (reluctant) efforts to establish child labor laws, protect children in courts of law (juvenile courts), and the Maternal and Child Health program, legislated in 1921. America is committed to shelter her children from harm and safeguard conditions for their well-being. Certainly America's future is in her children.

The responsibility for the welfare of America's children mixes private and public legal obligations. Children have no legal standing; because they are not autonomous they thus have no protectable interests of their own. Their interests are protected by their parents or by the state. *Parens paterie* expects the state to protect their interests, while the doctrine of parental responsibility rests on the parental right to "establish a home and bring up children...according to the dictates of [their] own conscience."[40] America's earliest social welfare interventions on behalf of children were based on the parens paterie credo. One of the original purposes of the 1935 Aid to Dependent Children program protected the right of children to remain in their own homes by granting them financial assistance rather than removing children to orphanages if the cause of their distress was financial and their home was otherwise suitable. Until then, it was not unusual for a financially dependent child to be removed from the home and placed in an orphanage. While the federal government still maintains its concern for welfare of the child, states have considerable legal authority to protect their welfare under parens paterie.[41] Setting social priorities to improve the ability of families to protect the welfare of their children, including their financial welfare, are indeed laudable, but such efforts risk exploiting economically dependent children to achieve behavioral changes in their mothers. Ironically, only a small share of TANF families have an employed family member (see Figure 4.3).

The TANF legacy: TANF emerged from longstanding discontent with cash assistance to financially dependent children, a persistent effort to make poor families responsible for their children by insisting they work for their benefits, the failed effort to bring financially dependent families into the Supplemental Security Income program, and President Clinton's political determination to put his experiences with welfare reform in Arkansas into federal law. He indeed ended welfare as we had known it for almost 80 years, and as a result, he abandoned a cherished commitment to America's children. Figure 4.4 shows that the percent of children in poverty has gradually increased since TANF has become institutionalized.

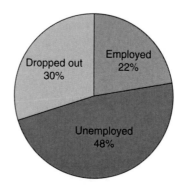

Figure 4.3   Employment status TANF families
Source: TANF Tenth Annual Report to Congress.

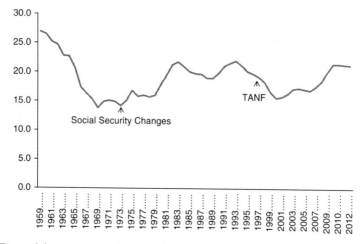

Figure 4.4   Percentage of children in poverty
Source: Data from US Bureau of the Census.

In a perverse way, TANF punishes children if their parents are unable or otherwise do not provide for their economic welfare. If the well being of children remains important to Americans, TANF is simply wrong-headed. TANF pandered to Republican rhetoric contained in Newt Gingrich's "Contract with America," confirmed that welfare dependency is not reduced by work, and has had little or no impact on reducing poverty, particularly among children. TANF also demonstrated the structural deficiencies in America's cash assistance programs, requiring the infusion of $5 billion of emergency funding in 2008–09. The final failure of TANF might be found in the irony that the TANF legislation required states to report if the child poverty rate increased by five percent or more as a result of that state's TANF program. However, the US Administration for Children and Families reports, "to date [2009], no State has been required to submit a corrective action plan or any additional information for these child poverty assessment periods."[42] Finally, TANF ends the long-standing commitment to provide economic security for financially dependent children.[43] Figure 4.4 shows the poverty rate among children began to rise after TANF lost its shock value, returning to its pre-TANF levels.

CONCLUSION

Supplemental Security Income and TANF are the two cash support assistance programs administered under the authority of the Social Security Act, which together with the two cash support insurance programs—Social Security and unemployment insurance—constitute the majority of the nation's cash support commitments. Neither SSI nor TANF contribute to the reduction of poverty, and both insult the capacity of American capitalism to provide for those in economic need. Constructed on shifting ideological sands, both SSI and TANF failed to bring economic relief to those under the pressure of the Great Recession. Neither they nor their predecessor programs ever showed the capacity to reduce poverty, and efforts to bring these programs up to poverty-level standards were never seriously considered.

TANF pretends a social welfare commitment devoid of any statutory right for poor children to receive their benefits. Instead, it has become a means to coerce the poor into behaving in extra-legal, socially desirable ways. Single mothers with dependent children are required to work, even in low-wage jobs, in order to receive TANF benefits for their children. Under such conditions, the larger structural issues, such as an economy that cannot produce adequate jobs, are never addressed. TANF also shows how presumed welfare savings in one program simply transfers the burden to other programs like SNAP (see Figure 4.5).

Figure 4.6 compares cash support from Social Security and cash support from SSI and TANF. Clearly both cash support assistance programs provide benefits well below the poverty line and well below Social

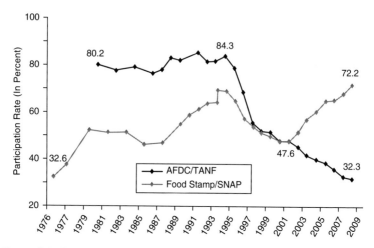

Figure 4.5 Participation rates in AFDC/TANF, Food Stamp/SNAP Programs, selected years

Source: Congressional Budget Office, 2007.

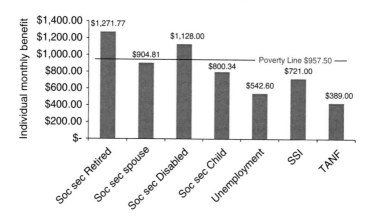

Figure 4.6 Average single-person monthly benefit payments by selected cash support programs

Source: Social Security Cash Support Programs (Author's calculation, sources vary).

Security. Today, 20 percent of the nation's children are poor, a percentage that has remained constant since before and after TANF was created. Only 28 percent of TANF funds are actually used for cash assistance to children and their families. While SSI represented a step toward developing a universal cash assistance program for those unable to work, it did so by excluding children and their adult caretakers from a systematic, more uniform method of providing cash support assistance benefits to them.

America's reluctance to protect its aged and disabled who are unable to work embodies its ideological disdain of poverty; her failure to take care of her children epitomizes America's shame. Both SSI and TANF cash support assistance programs require a legitimate foundation capable of directing their resources toward the problems of poverty. Since SSI is now administered under the authority of the Social Security Administration, this program offers the opportunity for greater integration with Social Security. TANF has failed to reduce poverty among children, and it needs to be dismantled. Repairing America's social welfare obligation to her children will require a recommitment to the value she has always held for the tenderest members of her society.

5. Supplemental Nutrition Assistance Program and the Earned Income Tax Credit ✑

INTRODUCTION

Puritan work ethics proved alive and well when economist James M. Buchanan, a Nobel Memorial Prize winner, alleged in 1994 that work is an ethical principle, not a personal or structural economic one. Buchanan contended that a person who avoids work, and the taxable income that could be earned by it, places greater obligations on others, for which that person carries a moral liability. When people work, according to Buchanan, they benefit others as well as themselves, while a "non-Puritan set of moral norms or constraints...may be unproductive and may actually reduce value in the economy" making everyone worse off as a result.[1] Idleness, according to Buchanan is morally wrong, because even the slightest amount of work brings a benefit to all. Buchanan's assertions simply buttressed growing consensus among conservative politicians who believed work was "redemptive" and "would rescue welfare recipients from the companions of sloth, including booze, idleness, illicit sex and hanging out."[2]

By 1994, enforced work by welfare recipients was well on its way to becoming the preferred way to reduce poverty. Both the Supplemental Nutrition Assistance Program (SNAP—formerly Food Stamps, 1963) and the Earned Income Tax Credit (EITC, 1973) were in place, and by 1994, both had become necessary cash support social welfare staples for those who worked but were still poor. These two programs are the third class of cash support programs discussed in the introductory chapter and summarized in Figure I.1.

SNAP began as an alternative program to utilize surplus foods by granting stamps, or vouchers, which could be exchanged for food, for poverty level or low-income people. With its gradual separation from distributing surplus foods, SNAP has lurched toward a program of cash support, and as it has expanded, SNAP has begun to build work requirements into its eligibility standards. Today SNAP has been expanded into a debit card that can be used to buy food, whether farm surplus food or not.[3] It provides benefits to low-income households and households including workers as long as their gross household income is less than 130 percent of federal poverty guidelines and their net income is less than 100 percent of the poverty guidelines.[4]

From its origin as a tax credit for low-income workers, EITC moved quickly to provide a cash rebate to workers whose tax liability was greater than the taxes they owed, a refundable tax credit, and form of a guaranteed income for selected low-income workers. EITC has always required work as a condition of receiving benefits. As EITC has been expanded incrementally it has become an important source of cash reimbursement to low-income workers, mostly those with children.

Neither program has a social welfare pedigree, but both EITC and SNAP have become programs that are no longer food or tax programs either. They contrast with the social insurances that provide benefits to people who have worked sufficiently to build up benefits they receive when they are not working, and they differ from the cash support assistance programs that are designed to provide benefits to those who are not expected to work.[5] SNAP and EITC are tethered to work, but unlike the social insurances and the cash assistance programs, neither SNAP nor EITC, for the most part, was developed as cash support programs for the poor or those with low income. Instead, both programs owe their emergence as social welfare programs to the inability of both the social insurances and the cash assistance programs to provide above-poverty-level benefits to those who were working but fell outside eligibility for the social insurances, or in the case of SNAP, those who might be receiving social insurances or other forms of cash assistance but were still in need of food benefits.

As they have gradually moved beyond their respective policy origins, both EITC and SNAP have pursued a social welfare foundation in America's traditional value of work, rather than in the value of economic security. Although all three categories of cash support are secured in one way or another by work, work as the social welfare fallback policy foundation for SNAP and EITC raises question about the American economic system, which cannot generate work that keeps people above poverty, and the extent to which present efforts to support work are capable of lifting people out of poverty. This chapter discusses why these programs were created, how they have become poverty-reducing programs, how the Great Recession exposed their failure as social welfare programs, and why these programs cry out for reorganization if they are to meet poverty-reducing social welfare objectives.

WORK AND POVERTY

The policy ambiguities of both SNAP and EITC rest in part on the contemporary understanding of work. Work in the American system today is not as easily understood as it might have been for the founding Puritans. On the individual level, work in the American system has become a normative concept rather than an ethical one, depending on one's own definition of work. An informative event in the evolution of Americans' understanding of work surfaced in the decades following WWII. As women-as-homemakers and as men-as-breadwinners gradually lost its appeal as the preferred family form, women began to assert that their efforts rearing children and creating a nurturing home environment were indeed work, and they declared that it be considered in computing benefits for Social Security. The contention was not without merit, particularly when the argument was couched in terms of homemaking as *productive* work.[6]

Contemporary work has other normative attributes. Americans are identified by their work, and what they do for a living often defines their social standing. It is not unusual to ask a stranger on first meeting, "What do you do?" Americans also hold an aesthetic value of work beyond its economic value, referred to as "workmanship." The value of labor is not limited by the amount of labor necessary to create a product, but by the quality of the labor that creates the product itself. An otherwise commonplace product like an automobile may be more highly valued for its beauty than for its utility, due to the quality of care and attention invested by labor to create the product. Even the most humble form of work is esteemed for is quality, and even the most mundane and unattractive forms of labor often are valued when that work is of high quality. Employment at any level is socially esteemed compared with unemployment, which is scorned, perhaps evidenced by the vast amount of labor provided by retired people in the form of voluntarism. Beliefs, aesthetic principles, social values, and personal economic self-interest—not moral ethics—drive the conviction that everyone in America should work, a judgment shared no less by the poor than by others.[7]

Even though work retains some foundation in individualism, it is greatly complicated by today's social and economic environment. As discussed in Chapter 2, employment decisions are most often impersonally made by the business, for reasons of profit, or as a result of larger economic events like the Great Recession. Hiring and firing are unlikely to stem from worker-employer relationships. Wages and the value of labor have become disconnected. The Great Recession caused the loss of jobs and massive loss of wealth. Globalization has exported jobs. Advanced mechanization has reduced the need for labor. Some may argue that there is a general aversion to work among the poor that can only be overcome by threats and punishment, but this view overlooks the economic structural vicissitudes that contribute to unemployment and poverty.

Above all, the structure of the American economy creates conditions in which work does not pay enough to keep workers out of poverty. The US Department of Labor reported that in 2011, about 22.5 percent of the poor were working at least 27 weeks during the year, although not necessarily working in consecutive months. In other words, approximately 7 percent of the entire American labor force was working but still fell below the poverty level. The numbers of poor people who cycle in and out of work during any year, but who work less than 27 weeks, is difficult to document, but the Department of Labor estimates that as many as 39 percent of the working poor may have been unemployed at least some time during the year and unable to find a steady job. The percentages of working poor in the national labor force are higher for women (8%), African Americans (13.3%), high school dropouts (20.1%), and families maintained by women (27.2%). The working poor are concentrated in low-wage jobs, mostly in the service sector, where wages, and/or numbers of hours worked, are not sufficient to keep them out of poverty.[8] These are difficult jobs for more reasons than their low wages. They are often sporadic, the employees are likely to have health problems, the working conditions are awful, the work hours are intermittent and typically unpredictable, and the workers likely need social supports for productive employment, such as transportation and child or older adult substitute care. These workers are the working poor: those who earn wages at or below the hourly wage that would give a family of four enough income to reach but not exceed the poverty threshold, given full-time, full-year work.

The National Employment Law Project provides contemporary perspectives on structural economic factors that also contribute to the poverty of people who are still working. Noting that low-wage jobs accounted for only 22 percent of job losses during the 2008–12 economic downturn, low-wage jobs represented 44 percent of jobs gained over the past 4 years:

> The food services and drinking places, administrative and support services (including temporary help), and retail trade industries are leading private sector job growth during the recent recovery phase. These [three] industries [alone], which pay relatively low wages, accounted for 39 percent of the private sector employment increase over the past four years.[9]

The food and beverage industry had the lowest hourly pay in any employment group at $9.48 per hour in 2013. In 2011, 28 percent of workers earned poverty-level wages (or $11.06 or less an hour), up from 23.1 percent in 2002. The average wage among these poverty-wage workers was $8.66 an hour versus $25.85 for all other workers.[10]

The increase of the working poor corresponded with rising income inequality in the United States. In the 12th edition of *The State of Working America* Lawrence Mishel, Josh Bivens, Elise Gould, and Heidi Shierholz compared the actual poverty rate with a simulated poverty rate based on a model of the statistical relationship between growth in per capita gross domestic product (GDP) and poverty from 1959 and 2010. Their model forecasts poverty quite accurately through the mid-1970s. When the country got richer, jobs paid relatively more, and poverty declined. If this relationship between per capita GDP growth and poverty had continued, they argue, the poverty rate would have fallen to zero by the 1980s. They conclude:

> Economic growth and poverty reduction clearly became decoupled in the mid-1970s, just as income inequality was taking off. As income inequality grows, poverty rates become less responsive to overall growth, because too little of that growth reaches the lower end of the income scale. Therefore, economic growth is a necessary factor in, but not sufficient for, broadly shared prosperity. Faster productivity growth, which creates more income per hour worked, provides the potential for significant poverty reduction, but only if that income reaches the lower end of the income scale. An underappreciated way to ensure that income reaches those at the bottom is to sustain genuinely full employment by targeting the absolutely lowest unemployment rate consistent with non-accelerating inflation.[11]

The two previous chapters discussed the limitations of social insurance programs and the cash support assistance programs to reduce or at least contain poverty within the environment of America's working poor. Both

EITC and SNAP propose to mitigate poverty for those who are working. Unfortunately, neither program has proved adequate to cushion the individual economic hardship of those who were working during the Great Recession or subsequently. EITC failed completely as its benefits were lost when jobs were lost; SNAP had the capacity to blunt personal economic hardship if eligibility levels had been more generous.[12] It is important to note, particularly in the Great Recession, that even with America's ability and authority to achieve a robust economy, these two programs in particular have substituted for the nation's efforts to achieve a full employment economy, or to make income from work sufficient to prevent or reduce poverty. With all of capitalism's emphasis on work, when work is not adequate to keep workers out of poverty, it seems disparaging of American capitalism.

EARNED INCOME TAX CREDIT

The Earned Income Tax Credit (EITC) is wrapped up in America's work enigma. EITC recognizes the importance of work's economic importance to the worker, but it also confirms that low-wage income from work does not produce sufficient economic value to keep people out of poverty. EITC concedes that taxes levied on work reduce its economic value, and that a progressive tax system should not contribute to poverty. By adding to the economic value of work, EITC presumes to encourage work and restrain poverty. EITC reflects an effort to assuage the problems of macroeconomic decisions with microeconomic solutions. EITC echoes other political adjustments to neoclassical economics discussed in Chapter 2, which are necessitated by social and economic changes, as when mechanization or globalization reduces labor's value. EITC has become a preferred way to mitigate low-wage employment through government subsidies, even though there may be other ways to enhance the economic value of work, such as an above-poverty minimum wage, enhanced rewards for work such as free lunches or free child care, or a heightened sense of prestige for work well done. EITC has developed into a politically valued but highly complex cash support initiative. Liberal and conservative social welfare commentators generally speak favorably of EITC. For liberals, EITC provides financial relief for workers in low-wage employment, improving their overall economic position and sometimes reducing poverty. To conservative observers, EITC encourages work, particularly in low-wage jobs.

Background: Congress created EITC as part of the Revenue Act of 1975, largely to offset the burden of Social Security taxes on low-income taxpayers during the 1974 economic downturn. Thus, EITC took its original form from tinkering with Social Security financing, some of which was discussed in Chapter 3. EITC's original modest program of cash support for low-wage workers who had dependent children has been expanded on a number of occasions, most notably by the Tax Reform Act of 1986. The 2009 American Recovery and Reinvestment Act (ARRA) continued the EITC expansion to married couples and families with three or more children, and the Tax Relief Unemployment Insurance Reauthorization and Job Creation Act of 2010 extended the benefits through the 2013 tax-filing season and presently until at least 2018. Since its inception, 26 states have adopted similar EITC programs with similar state benefits added to those provided by the federal government contributing to the incremental expansion of a program first designed to lessen the tax burden on low-wage workers.

As a cash support program, EITC is a refundable tax credit administered through the Treasury Department. Although various forms of tax credits existed before 1975, EITC was the first *refundable* tax credit, meaning that a cash refund is provided to the taxpayer if the tax credit is greater than taxes owed. EITC put a new wrinkle in tax policy. Although EITC acts to reduce poverty, its political purpose is to encourage work in low-paying jobs. EITC might be thought of as a two-tiered program of cash support. The base program is a credit that is applied to income taxes owed as a result of employment. The second tier of the program is a cash refund if the credit is worth more than the taxes owed. Because earnings are the basis for computing the tax credit, people must be employed to receive it, and only earnings are counted toward the credit. The amount of the tax credit is based on a formula that takes into account the worker's wages, the number of children, and worker's marital status. The formula is constructed so that as wages rise, the amount of the credit increases until, at a certain level of earnings, the credit begins to decrease. Maximum earnings levels in 2013 topped out at $13,980 (not the amount of tax refund) for a single worker without children and up to $50,270 for a married couple with three or more children (see Box 5.1). In 2012, EITC paid out about $54 billion in tax refunds, which accounts for about 80 percent of the program's cost; the balance was made up in the amount of lost taxes.[13]

BOX 5.1   2014 EXPECTED EITC GUIDELINES*

The maximum amounts of the credit are $487 for taxpayers without children, $3,250 for taxpayers with one child, $5,372 for taxpayers with two children, and $6,044 for taxpayers with three or more children. (The credit amounts change each year with the price of goods and services, as measured by the consumer price index for all urban consumers.)

The credit begins to phase out when earnings (or adjusted gross income, if higher) are greater than $7,970 for taxpayers without children or $17,530 for taxpayers with children. Eligibility for the credit is cut off when income exceeds $14,340 for taxpayers without children, $37,870 for taxpayers with one child, $43,038 for taxpayers with two children, and $46,227 for taxpayers with three or more children. For married couples filing jointly, the cutoffs are extended by an additional $5,340. (Those income thresholds are also adjusted annually for inflation.)

* Congress of the United States, Congressional Budget Office, "Refundable Tax Credits," January 2013, p. 27.

EITC was based on the earlier idea of a negative income tax first introduced in 1960s as a guaranteed annual income (GAI) and in the 1970s as part of Daniel Moynihan's Family Assistance Plan (FAP), which resulted in the creation of Supplemental Security Income in 1974[14] (see Chapter 4). The roots of EITC were deeply set in the welfare reform skirmishes that made the proposed FAP unworkable for families and children. The fear that a guaranteed income would simply create "welfare dependency," especially expressed by Senator Russell Long, and Long's insistence that there be a form of "workfare" in any welfare reform, did little to discourage the Nixon administration from exploring negative income tax (NIT) proposals, a comprehensive study of the effect of a guaranteed income on work incentives,[15] and extensive studies by the Congressional Joint Economic Committee's through its "Studies in Public Welfare" initiatives.[16] For the most part, this vast literature favored some form of income guarantee to reduce the economic burden of poverty.

According to Dennis Ventry, the fallout from the failed FAP stimulated the Department of Health, Education and Welfare (DHEW) and the

Department of Labor (DOL) to revive support for some form of income guarantee as an option to the Aid to Families with Dependent Children welfare program, which the creation of Supplemental Security Income (SSI) left to stand alone. Unfortunately, perhaps reliving the history of the War on Poverty, HEW and DOL took different approaches to income guarantees. DHEW wanted an unencumbered cash transfer program similar to SSI, while the DOL wanted a program that encouraged labor force participation. At the same time, the Department of the Treasury had concluded that low-income earners were being taxed unfairly and recommended new tax adjustments accordingly. President Ford supported a tax credit for low-income workers as an economic stimulus by crafting EITC as a hybrid of income guarantee and work incentives. Russell Long agreed to support EITC as a way to divert low-income workers from applying for welfare programs.[17]

EITC differed significantly from the original NIT proposals because it was only available for people who worked and had income tax liability. It was not a guaranteed income. In this way, EITC presumed to encourage workforce participation for people likely to end up in low-paying jobs that they might be forced to take because of welfare eligibility criteria that required them to work. However, EITC faced problems similar to those that made an NIT unworkable. To focus tax credits on low-income workers, a formula had to be set that gradually phased out the value of the credits as earnings increased.[18] If the phase out was too steep its value as a work incentive would be modest and provide only a small work incentive. But a shallow phase out increased the size of the beneficiary pool and the cost of EITC in payments and lost taxes. Although EITC was originally restricted to workers who had children, the EITC beneficiary pool and the phase out formula have been expanded almost yearly in order to accommodate the income needs of low-income workers. The largest changes took place in 1986 when the program was opened to workers without children and when married two family workers received benefits based on both workers when filing taxes.

EITC best represents the challenge inherent in efforts to reduce poverty through ongoing incremental program additions to the social welfare system as a response to a specific economic problem without building a structurally sound social welfare base. EITC clearly began as a more modest decision to reduce taxes for the poor and to stimulate employment during an economic recession, with preference given to low-wage earners, yet its purpose became mixed as social welfare advocates saw it as a way to reduce poverty. In other words, initial support for EITC rested on its ability to "make work pay," thereby encouraging work as an alternative to welfare. But as it expanded government subsidies to workers in the form of tax credits and its cash refunds when credits exceeded allowable credits, EITC acquired strong poverty-reducing social welfare features. Eighty percent of the cost of the program now consists of the cash refunds made by the Treasury Department. While EITC embodies both poverty-reducing and work-motivation objectives, it functions poorly at meeting either. Advocates for "welfare reform" supported EITC because it purported to eliminate welfare[19] if, conservatives argued, EITC was not so generous that it undermined motivation to work, and if, liberals argued, EITC was sufficient to eliminate poverty. EITC has only marginally reached both objectives.[20] During the 2010 tax year, the average EITC payment was $2,805 for a family with children and $262 for a family without children.

EITC's Mixed Policy Expectations

The deliberate effort to combine cash assistance with tax reform as a means to enhance workforce participation puts EITC and its cousin, the Child Tax Credit, in a confusing social welfare policy environment. While EITC has had an effect on reducing poverty among the working poor, it raises serious questions about the way America has developed its social welfare programs and provides insights into why they have not been successful at reining in poverty. In some ways, EITC has tried to bridge economics and politics caught up in foundation structures of both as discussed in Chapter 2. Economically, EITC provides tax credits and cash to low-earning employed people in much the same way as FAP or NIT proposed in the early 1970s as a way to keep people working in lieu of structural economic changes. In this view, EITC is a social welfare patch on a wound of the economic system. The value of both the tax credits and cash have not been sufficient enough to reduce poverty significantly among the working poor; therefore, it perpetuates the problem of low-wage employment, resulting in frequent EITC expansions.

EITC has had a small effect on reducing poverty, and in a perverse way, it may perpetuate low-income employment. Using the Supplemental Poverty Measure, which measured poverty at 16 percent in 2010 (see Chapter 1), Mishel, Bivens, Gould, and Shierholz concluded that without EITC, poverty would have been 18 percent, and without SNAP it would been 17.2 percent, providing further evidence that these programs have a minor effect on reducing poverty as they are currently provided. They concluded that improved wages are the best way to reduce poverty among the working poor: "A weak job market greatly curtails the effectiveness of these [economic] supports." Furthermore, from 1979 through 2007, they show that as earned wages improved, spending on direct cash transfers and in-kind programs declined as percentages of family income for the bottom one-fifth of the income distribution scale, implying that higher earnings, not various cash transfer programs, are the best way to reduce poverty.[21]

To the extent that EITC does nothing to encourage the development of better-paying jobs, and it provides little in the way of alleviating poverty, its value as a social welfare program is limited. Economically, EITC accepts the fact that employment, even full-time employment, does not provide sufficient income to keep people out of poverty. A tax credit approach to solving a social welfare problem simply shifts the burden of providing cash support to the Treasury Department and embroils EITC in debates over the larger economic benefits of tax credits. Politically, EITC's work incentive value is subject to the same "notch" problems that plagued both FAP and later President Carter's Better Jobs and Income welfare reform proposals. EITC's tax credits may provide incentives that encourage people to work in low-paying jobs, but they require a balance between a work incentive and benefit adequacy in order to keep work motivation high without undermining the competitive value of private sector work. Since people choose to work for a variety of reasons, financial adequacy alone may not provide sufficient reason to continue working at low-income employment. Because there is no outright income guarantee, EITC and other refundable tax credits stretch the tax system into a cash distribution system, changing the character of the tax system without changing its basic, publically understood purposes of raising revenue, not giving it away.

Its macroeconomic features do not compensate for EITC's microeconomic complications, either. One might argue that if the American economic system cannot provide jobs and/or jobs that pay enough, the federal government has the obligation and capacity to subsidize employment. Such an argument, however, raises issues as to how government subsidization is accomplished so that public funds are used on behalf of the public. EITC certainly falls short of answering this kind of question. EITC does not discriminate among those private sector employments that may have public benefit from those that may not, nor does it take into account any return on investment of federal funds from private sector employers, advantages that accrue to the employers as a result of EITC. The willingness of government to support low-wage employment certainly enhances the value of the employer by keeping labor costs low and profits high. EITC adds financial value to the firm for which it is not expected to account. There are, of course, other ways to subsidize low-income employment that has value to the entire economy. Public projects are one means to subsidize employment, whether funded and administered by the federal government or contracted out to public or private firms. And there are certainly other ways to motivate people to work in low-paying jobs, such as better contractual support for labor unions[22] and insistence on minimum wages that are above poverty-level.[23] EITC fails to put some of the share of the cost of low-income employment back on the shoulders of the employer, and without setting its benefits at poverty-level wages, as a social welfare program might be likely to do, EITC's benefits do not assure its ability to reduce poverty (see Table 5.1).

Administrative issues: Creating a social welfare program like EITC within the Internal Revenue Service was bound to raise problems: the Internal Revenue code is complex enough, without saddling it with a means-tested social welfare burden. At the same time, adjusting a social welfare program to IRS rules has created administrative problems. The Joint Economic Committee of Congress recently estimated that 21 to 25 percent of the EITC payments made in fiscal year 2012 were paid in error, and that the IRS conducts over 500,000 EITC audits per year. Seventy percent of these audits withheld EITC payments until audits were completed, saving the federal government approximately $2.1 billion in 2012. According to the committee, "EITC taxpayers are disproportionately subject to audit, and they are twice as likely to be audited as other taxpayers. For FY 2011 EITC audits were 31 percent

Table 5.1 Maximum EITC payment by tax year and number of qualifying children

Number of Qualifying Children	Year			
	2009 ($)	2010 ($)	2011 ($)	2012 ($)
Three or more qualifying children	5,657	5,666	5,751	5,891
Two qualifying children	5,028	5,036	5,112	5,236
One qualifying child	3,043	3,050	3,094	3,169
No qualifying children	457	457	464	475

Source: Joint Economic Committee, January 2014.

of all individual audits."[24] The Department of the Treasury's Inspector General for Tax Administration explained the administrative problem with EITC:

> EITC eligibility rules are complicated and cause taxpayers to make errors while attempting to interpret and apply the tax laws to their individual situations. In addition, the changing population of taxpayers who claim the EITC increases the difficulty the IRS faces in improving EITC compliance. The IRS has conducted numerous studies showing how taxpayers move in and out of the EITC program. Studies show that approximately one-third of EITC claimants each year are intermittent or first-time claimants. The Department of the Treasury stated that none of the six factors listed above can be considered the primary driver of EITC improper payments. The interaction among the factors makes it extremely difficult to address the credit's improper payment rate while balancing the need to ensure that eligible taxpayers receive the credit.[25]

Summary: For all of its benefits, EITC complicates other cash support initiatives for poverty-level and low-income earners. Based on *earned* income, work incentive features expose an underlying social welfare weakness that attaches eligibility for cash support to people who are working, usually referred to as the working poor, and these standards have remained consistently below poverty thresholds. Moreover, EITC shifts the economic burden of low-income employment to the federal government, and where it exists, to state governments. While it may find macroeconomic justification, EITC fails to address the structural economic conditions that make it necessary in the first place. In this respect, an increase in the minimum wage to poverty levels as well as lowering the number of hours worked per week to "full-time" status would in itself reduce the need for EITC at best, and at least shift some of the economic burden of low wages back to the employer.

CHILD TAX CREDITS

The EITC has been linked with the child tax credit (CTC), although it has developed on a slightly different basis. The CTC was the second refundable tax credit, created by the Taxpayers Relief Act in 1997. Like EITC, the CTC increases as earnings rise, up to the maximum of $1,000 per child, and like the EITC, it reduces tax rates in its phase-in range and at higher income levels until the credit is gradually reduced. However, EITC begins to phase in with the first dollar of earnings, but earners eligible for the CTC wait until they have earned at least $3,000. The credit tops out at $1,000, the maximum credit amount, and a cash refund for workers with little or no tax up to a maximum of $1,000 per child under the age of 17. The CTC begins to phase out when adjusted gross income (with some modifications) reaches $75,000.[26]

BOX 5.2   CHILD TAX CREDIT

Reduces taxes of low- and moderate-income taxpayers with children under the age of 17 and provides cash assistance to workers who owe little or no income tax.

The child tax credit equals the smaller of taxpayers' income tax liability before credits and the maximum credit amount ($1,000 per child). However, workers with little or no tax liability before the credit are eligible for a refundable amount (referred to in the tax code as the "additional" child tax credit). For each additional dollar of earnings above $3,000, the refundable portion of the credit rises by 15 cents until the credit reaches a maximum of $1,000 per child under the age of 17.

Taxpayers with three or more children can choose another method to calculate the additional credit. Under that alternative, the credit equals the amount by which their share of payroll taxes exceeds the earned income tax credit. They can claim the larger of the credit amounts determined under the two alternative approaches.

The child tax credit begins to phase out when adjusted gross income (with some modifications) reaches $75,000 for a single filer or a head of household ($110,000 for a married couple filing jointly).

Source: Congressional Budget Office, 2013.

The Congressional Budget Office estimates that without EITC, 3.1 million more children would have been poor in 2011, lifting the poverty rate for children to well over 30 percent, and that without supplementing the earnings of low-paid workers with EITC and CTC, an additional 9.4 million people, including 4.9 million children, would have been poor in 2011, raising the overall poverty rate to well over 25 percent, in 2011 under the federal government's Supplemental Poverty Measure, which counts noncash public benefits and refundable tax credit payments as poverty-reducing resources. The Child Tax Credit faces some of the same policy problems and administrative complexity as EITC does.

SUPPLEMENTAL NUTRITION ASSISTANCE PROGRAM

The Supplemental Nutrition Assistance Program (SNAP, formerly Food Stamps) has a long history that reflects a program built on an outdated foundation, and like the other cash support programs discussed above, SNAP has been tinkered with and modified in efforts to keep it relevant to the needs of the today's poor, but has had little success at eliminating or significantly reducing poverty.

SNAP's main objective today is to make sure that the poor have nutritious food. The program originated in 1939 as a way to help those still recovering from the Great Depression to purchase US government surplus food.[27] Pre- and post-Depression efforts to stabilize farming used federal funds to buy farm products or to encourage farmers to limit production of certain crops. Thus, the earliest food stamp program granted $0.50 in free stamps for each $1.00 worth of food stamps that were purchased. The stamps then could be used to purchase foods released from those stored in federal warehouses. As the Great Depression wound down, so did this food stamp program; instead, surplus government foods were offered to nonprofit organization and welfare recipients without charge after the program came to an end in 1943. The idea of providing food stamps that allowed low-income people to buy selected foods in local markets, instead of distributing commodity foods, was revived by Representative Lenore K. Sullivan (D. MO), and in 1961, President Kennedy began a limited program under an executive order, since there was legislative authority for the program but it was never implemented by President Eisenhower. The program became official in 1964. The Food Stamp program has been changed repeatedly since then, and changes to the program in 2008 also gave it its present name: SNAP.

SNAP has been politically fused with agriculture from its very beginning, and continues to be inescapably linked to farm legislation. This is the reason the Department of Agriculture's agency, Food, and Nutrition Services (FNS) administers it. Representative Sullivan, from urban Saint Lewis, won support for food stamps by tying her support for continued farm subsidies, supported by rural constituencies, with Food Stamp legislation that appealed to urban constituents. Efforts to wrestle the Food Stamp Program away from the Agricultural Committee and make it part of an income maintenance block grant proved the move that finally sank the welfare reform proposed by President Carter in 1978–79.[28] Agriculture balked at putting food stamps into the block grant, even though the Chairman of the House Ways and Means Committee was somewhat favorably disposed to the idea.

> One [Department of Agriculture] staffer commented. "Agriculture needs an urban base." Farming makes up such a small portion of agriculture spending today, and that of our constituency, that without urban spending, agriculture would be lost. And you need to remember…welfare is big business, not so much in the amount we spend for benefits, but who carries out the programs. In agriculture, grocery stores are big beneficiaries of food stamps, as are those in the computer industry who are developing debit card type spending mechanisms, and those who are constantly investigating fraud. Food stamps are big business, and agriculture had to hang on to them.[29]

SNAP, like EITC, is a hybrid cash support program for several reasons. As noted above, SNAP does not provide cash directly, but issues a debit card that can be used to purchase approved foods. While SNAP is available to people in households with income less than 130 percent of the poverty level, it does not necessarily consider itself a program for low-income people, but rather it is promoted for people experiencing "food insecurity." SNAP beneficiaries may also be working, but are not required to be. Table 5.2 shows that 30 percent of the households have earned income that averages $1,174.00 per month, and when added to the average SNAP benefit, places a two person household at approximately 125 percent of the poverty level. At the same time, however, the 60 percent of SNAP beneficiaries with unearned income of an average of $858.00 per month realize an average of $265.00 SNAP benefit amounting to about $2,000.00 below the poverty level for a two-person family. Whereas SNAP may help keep some households marginally above the poverty line, approximately 60 percent of SNAP beneficiaries remain in poverty. The maximum SNAP benefit averages out at $5.15 per person per day for food and is unlikely to keep many individuals out of poverty.

SNAP has a two-tiered eligibility standard: categorical and income eligibility. Persons who are recipients of cash assistance programs are automatically eligible for SNAP benefits. Income eligibility calculates gross income, 130 percent of the poverty line, and net income, available

Table 5.2 Summary of the SNAP program

	Participating Households		Average Gross	
	Number (Millions)	Percentage	Monthly Income ($)	Average Monthly SNAP Benefit ($)
Households with different types of people				
With children	8.9	49	923	419
With people age 60 or older	2.9	16	813	144
With disabled people age 59 or younger	3.6	20	946	219
Without children, people age 60 or older, or disabled people	4.3	24	268	194
Households with different types of income				
Earned income	5.5	30	1,174	343
No earned income	12.9	70	542	263
Unearned income	11.1	60	858	265
Social Security income	3.9	21	948	164
Supplemental Security Income	3.8	21	863	212
TANF income	1.5	8	719	428
No income	3.6	20	0	297
All Households	18.4	100		287
All Persons	45.7	100	731	Per Day 5.15

Source: Congressional Budget Office based on Esa Eslami, Kai Filion, and Mark Strayer, *Characteristics of Supplemental Nutrition Assistance Program Households: Fiscal Year 2010* (report submitted by Mathematica Policy Research to the Department of Agriculture, Food and Nutrition Service, Office of Research and Analysis, September 2011).

spendable income when deductions such as child care, transportation to work, and other factors states may consider are reduced from the gross income. Assets over approximately $2,000.00 will also make households ineligible for benefits. Approximately 75 percent of households qualify for SNAP categorically.

SUMMARY

SNAP eligibility is not restricted to workers who have earnings, unlike EITC, and unlike EITC SNAP has important countercyclical features and thus is likely to respond to contemporary economic structural issues. This is the good news about SNAP. The Congressional Budget Office stated:

> Between 2007 and 2011, both the number of people eligible for SNAP and the rate at which eligible people claimed benefits increased. Labor market conditions deteriorated dramatically between 2007 and 2009 and have been slow to recover: The unemployment rate jumped from 4.6 percent in 2007 to 9.6 percent in 2010 and was still at 8.5 percent at the end of 2011. The number of people eligible for the program increased by an estimated 20 percent from 2007 to 2009 (the latest year for which such data are available) and probably at an even faster rate from 2009 to 2011.[30]

The bad news is that SNAP is locked into agriculture, and as long as it is, SNAP will be challenged to find its social welfare foundation. As SNAP has expanded into a hybrid cash support program, it has been pushed back to into a traditional social welfare structure, namely that benefits must be tied to work, when, as with EITC, it has become clearer and clearer that one's relationship to work in the American system is no longer a personal individual one. Of course, insisting that welfare benefits such a SNAP be dependent on work, when there is no work, or when work does not pay enough to keep people from needing SNAP benefits, is a subtle way of keeping social welfare commitments to a minimum and perpetuating the income inequality that has grown more serious in America. This anti-welfare message was quite clear in recent testimony about the 2014 Farm Bill:

> A final way to save money in the SNAP program is to strengthen the program's work requirements. Indeed, more Americans must work and earn all or most of their household income if federal and state governments are to move in the direction of fiscal solvency. The current SNAP program has work requirements that look strong on paper. These include the requirement that non-disabled and non-elderly recipients register for work, accept a job if offered, search for work or meet other work requirements that states impose (and are approved by the Department of Agriculture). In addition, recipients cannot quit a job or voluntarily reduce their hours of work to less than 30.[31]

CONCLUSION

EITC and SNAP entered the social welfare mainstream as the War on Poverty failed to reduce poverty as its architects had anticipated. EITC originated from the recognition that economic opportunity, in itself, was not sufficient to lift the poor out of poverty, and those later efforts to establish a national income maintenance floor was compromised by concerns that a form of guaranteed income would discourage people from working. EITC created the first refundable tax credit, requiring the Internal Revenue Service to assume social welfare tasks. SNAP began by distributing surplus foods to the poor. SNAP's gradual transformation from a program limited to specific food to open-ended food purchases thrust it forward as a social welfare response to poverty highlighted during the Kennedy-Johnson presidencies. The political support for both programs depends on recipients' attachment to work in an economic environment where jobs are scarce, many available jobs pay less than poverty wages, and economic conditions have forced many otherwise employable people out of the labor force. Neither program satisfies social welfare economic security objectives in such an economic environment. In a perverse way, EITC in particular might perpetuate poverty by supplementing low-wage private sector employment.

Both programs are plagued with administrative problems. Both are hybrid programs of their respective administrative agencies. Neither the Department of the Treasury nor the Department of Agriculture have sufficient social welfare experience to allow them to administer either program in such a way that the cash assistance they offer can be effective at reducing poverty. The problem the Department of the Treasury noted, of blending refundable tax credits and income supplements for low-wage employment, is more than enough to suggest that even if EITC is the right kind of poverty-reducing program and could be effective, its implementation rests with the wrong agency. Blending providing food to low-income people with agricultural policy has always been questionable, and with the growing disconnect between farm subsidies and support for those in poverty, the antipoverty value of SNAP has been held hostage to agricultural issues, as the recent farm bill illustrates. SNAP simply is in the wrong place, even if it were a proven poverty-reducing program.

From a social welfare policy perspective, EITC in particular fails to reduce poverty significantly and does not have the capacity to protect individuals from loss of income during periods of structural economic distress. When work fails, so does EITC. In fact, EITC might perpetuate low-income employment. There are other ways to "make work pay." Moreover, to the extent that it is economically, socially, and politically desirable to make sure that everyone who is able has a job that pays above poverty wages, government as the employer of last resort provides a better policy option than EITC.

In the final analysis, bringing both programs into closer harmony with the social insurances and the cash support assistance programs can enhance their anti-poverty value. This option is discussed further in the final chapter.

Part III   Integration of Social Welfare and the American Economy to Reduce Poverty ❧

6. Developing a New Social Welfare Structure ❧

INTRODUCTION

America's present-day economic system has failed many of its most needy, and as it has tilted into the twenty-first century, it has eroded formative values of democracy as well. The Great Recession evidenced America's greatest economic collapse since the Great Depression of 1929–34, and while the political actions undertaken to rescue capitalism restored private economic institutions, they bypassed millions who lost their income security. The social welfare programs first crafted 80 years ago to prevent or cushion personal economic calamity when America's economic system failed confirmed their inadequacy to protect middle- and low-income people during this most recent economic crisis, just as the same programs have failed to reduce poverty over the past 50 years. American capitalism was unprepared for the Great Recession, and the existing social welfare network proved unable to provide relief from its economic damage to many, offering an unvarnished view of its poverty-reducing insufficiencies. The economy may be showing signs of improvement, but millions are struggling to drag themselves out of personal economic ruin.

American capitalism today is far removed from the economic principles proposed by Adam Smith and massaged by neo-capitalist economists since. The Great Depression's economic shock, followed by World War II, forced America away from capitalism's classic economic activity and into the macroeconomic world of fiscal planning. The Employment Act of 1946 gave America the capacity and the authority to manage her economy in order to achieve economic growth, economic balance, and economic justice. The new economic muscle driven by Keynesian economics began a shift away from personal economic choices toward a system where economic choices that affect individuals are made through third party, anonymous decision makers, a problem of "agency" according to Joseph Stiglitz. Individuals are likely to be hired and fired by "the firm," not by an individual owner; individual financial investment decisions are made through mutual funds, and macroeconomic decisions such as keeping inflation low, for example, result in persistent unemployment. In other words, individuals participate in the economy through agents, rather than directly.

The failure of America's social welfare system to protect Americans from the country's present economic fallout exposes the same root problems as the failure of American capitalism leading up to the Great Recession. Individual decision-making has given way to a broader economic and social environment. Nineteenth-century economic structures simply are not sufficient to provide robust American economic development. Likewise, the present social welfare system is unable to protect Americans caught up in economic circumstances they are unable to control. To argue that social welfare policy represents individual choices while macroeconomic decisions represent reasoned economic planning robs the potential of both. Social welfare and American capitalism are not competitors but have become intermixed in the world of twenty-first-century America. The belief that successful economic markets work through an invisible hand, that laissez-faire government encourages economic justice, and that people maximize their economic future through their own choices, is just as foreign to the way American capitalism operates today as the belief that work is the solution to poverty and that the unemployment that causes the need for social welfare support is a personal choice. American capitalism no longer rests on individual economic decisions, nor is poverty simply a matter of bad choices.

Perhaps a recent statement by Janet Yellen sums up efforts to balance employment problems with larger economic objectives:

> The large shortfall of employment relative to its maximum level has imposed huge burdens on all too many American households and represents a substantial social cost. In addition, prolonged economic weakness could harm the economy's productive potential for years to come.... With employment so far from its maximum level and with inflation running below the [Federal Reserve's] 2 percent objective, I believe it's appropriate for progress in the labor market to take center stage in the conduct of monetary policy.[1]

Both social welfare and American capitalism have been patched and juggled to keep them running without the resolve to reset their foundations in the new realities of both. The net result has left the economy weaker, and produced unnecessary economic suffering for vast numbers of average people, and most shamefully, these patched-up systems have allowed the poverty of the nineteenth and twentieth centuries, unchecked for almost 100 years, to continue unbridled into twenty-first-century America.

Our nation has the resources, the legal authority, and the institutional capacity to confront her poverty more honestly and effectively should she choose to do so. A new economic model—one containing more government economic management—will require a partner social welfare system capable of providing economic security to her people as the national economy moves beyond its nineteenth-century assumptions.

A New Social Welfare Paradigm

It appears something has gone wrong with America's economic engine; it has created the most robust economy in the world, but leaves almost a quarter of its children in poverty. Clearly, the persistence of American poverty goes well beyond personal economic hardship. Moreover, poverty inflicts social penalties on those above the official poverty line as well as those in the very bottom of the poverty population. Deteriorating neighborhoods, poor performing schools, increased crime, family disintegration, and a general social malaise are some of the larger social conditions long associated with poverty. In their highly detailed book, Richard Wilkinson and Kate Pickett present startling relationships between national income inequality and a wide array of social indicators. The correlation between income inequality in the United States and an index of poor health, social problems, and percent of mental illness is greater than any of the industrialized nations in the world. Income inequality in the United States also correlates strongly with illiteracy, social immobility, excessive homicides, poor children, and trust in other people.[2]

There is no indication that present social welfare programs have been able to stem the growing tide of poverty brought about by the hangover of the Great Recession, and there are no redeeming social values associated with poverty. Furthermore, the consequence of American inequality and its persistent poverty extends beyond America's shores. Joseph Stiglitz is not alone when he cautions, "As democracies grow in many other parts of the world an economic and political system that leaves most citizens behind—as ours has been doing—will not be seen as a system to be emulated, and the rules of the game that such a country advocates will be approached with jaundiced eyes."[3]

An unprecedented increase in income inequality between the rich and the poor, as authoritatively documented by the Congressional Budget Office, has been coupled with persistent poverty in the United States:

> As a result of that uneven income growth, the distribution of after-tax household income in the United States was substantially more unequal in 2007 than in 1979. The share of income accruing to higher income households increased, whereas the share accruing to other households declined. In fact, between 2005 and 2007, the after-tax income received by the 20 percent of the population with the highest income exceeded the after-tax income inequality.[4]

The Gini Index, a measure of income inequality, now stands at 0.48, up from 0.37 a decade ago, showing a serious unequal income distribution in the United States, far greater than in any of the industrial nations.[5] This growth of income inequality also took place under the umbrella of restricted social spending. There is nothing in the lexicon of American social welfare that says that it should be an equalizer of wealth, but beyond protection of the individual from personal economic calamity, it does indeed carry out an important form of economic redistribution. Certainly the increase in America's income gap reflects economic choices that have shifted wealth for the benefit of the wealthy often at the expense of the poor. This does not seem to be what the Employment Act had in mind.

Addressing the larger political and economic context for reducing American poverty raises issues of broad-scale institutional reforms that go well beyond the scope of this discussion. Instead, this chapter offers a more manageable approach to reducing American poverty within the framework of existing social welfare institutions. Based on evidence that social programs have expanded in scope, but their underlying political and economic structures have not been reformed to support these expansions, a social welfare enterprise based on twenty-first-century economic and political realities requires rebuilding the base of America's commitments.

Rebuilding the Base

This discussion deliberately has singled out the cash support programs for their ability to contain, reduce, and possibly eliminate poverty in America. The federal government now administers and funds six cash support programs that comprise almost all of the federal cash distributed to Americans. The responsibility for the present cash support network is authorized under three different legislative authorities and is parsed out to three different administrative agencies. The Social Security Act has authority for the social insurance programs (OASDI and UI), which account for about two-thirds of all federal cash outlays, and for the cash assistance programs of SSI and TANF, which constitute another 13 percent of cash outlays. EITC, administrated under the authority of the Internal Revenue Service, and SNAP, administered under the authority of the Department of Agriculture, account for the final 13 percent of federal cash outlays (see Figure I.1 in the Introduction). The cash support programs remain the base for a reformed social welfare system capable of protecting Americans from personal economic losses and ensuring that their incomes remain above poverty level.

The forgoing discussion has avoided an examination of the many social programs that impact the lives of poor people. Medicaid, public housing and assisted housing, the school lunch program, Pell grants, and various social services offered under the Social Services Block Grant and Child Welfare Block Grant, are a few among the many social programs alluded to in Chapter 1. The social resources available to poor people from these programs are important to help them find some stability in their lives, but they do not mitigate poverty. In many ways, these programs help stabilize the social landscape or provide a form of social parity for the poor. Without Medicaid, for example, the poor would have even less medical care, but Medicaid does not reduce poverty. Over the years, as social programs have been expanded, they have developed into a bewildering array of resources that may or may not be available to any individual person in poverty. The emergence of a complex mélange of programs has been driven by interest groups that have questionable significance for poor people. Present-day policy elites maintain command of policy debates over this vast array of services lest their status with economic and political decision-makers diminishes.

The many social changes in the lives of Americans have also been omitted from this discussion. The drastic changes in the nature of families as well as other startling developments in society, amply discussed by Jody Heymann and Allison Earle, raise questions not only about pervasive poverty, but also about the adequacy of America's social structures in general and their ability to adapt to these changing social conditions. Joseph Hacker's observations that "over the last generation economic risk has increasingly shifted from the broad shoulders of government and corporations onto the backs of American workers and their families" also signal calls for revamping America's social welfare commitments.[6] These and other contributions that lend alternate understandings of poverty and efforts to defy it suggest the need for comprehensive rethinking of the promotion of the welfare of all of its citizens and raises proposals beyond those for improving the system of cash support for the poor, the major focus of this book.

Changing the Foundation for the Cash Support Programs

All the cash support programs acknowledge an impact on keeping people out of poverty even though none of them have specific policies that do so. For example: Social Security claims to reduce poverty among the aged by 40 percent, claiming to reduce poverty overall by 21 percent. Unemployment insurance, too, claims to reduce poverty. The Congressional Budget Office reports, "The poverty rate for families in which someone was unemployed in 2009 was 19.6 percent. Without UI benefits, that rate would have been 4.7 percentage points higher, or 24.3 percent."[7]

"The value of food stamp benefits, *when added to cash income,*... boosted nearly 9 percent above poverty. Nearly one-fourth of a food stamp household's monthly income came from food stamps,"[8] the Department of Agriculture states. The Tax Policy Center claims that "the IRS estimates that in 2009, the [Earned Income Tax] credit lifted nearly 7 million people {approximately 12 percent} out of poverty."[9] To the extent that these estimates are reliable, without Social Security, EITC, SNAP, and unemployment insurance, America's poverty rate might reach as high as 53 percent! Certainly, however, cash support from social insurances and forms of cash support from assistance indeed reduce poverty, but perhaps not as much as these agencies claim.[10]

Unfortunately, today's cash support programs operate under different eligibility rules, weakening their overall effectiveness. For example, Social Security distributes cash to retirees, the disabled who have worked, and their family members; SNAP distributes its benefits to *households*; TANF distributes its benefits to *children in families*; SSI distributes its benefits to *individuals;* EITC distributes its benefits to *workers*. These different beneficiary criteria built incrementally over years of program development create a befuddling approach to distributing cash resources. Box 6.1 provides a typical example of the confusion caused by repeated incremental changes to the cash support programs in efforts to make them relevant without modifying the foundations upon which they were originally created.[11]

BOX 6.1   THE FOOD STAMP (SNAP) TANGLE*

Generally, your household cannot have more than $2,000 in resources (things you own). But, if your household includes a person age 60 or older or who is disabled, the limit is $3,000. Resources of people who receive Supplemental Security Income (SSI) or benefits under the Temporary Assistance for Needy Families (TANF) program are not counted for SNAP purposes. Resources include cash, bank accounts and other property.

Not all resources you own count. For example, your home and the land it is on do not count for SNAP eligibility. A car or truck counts differently depending on how it is used. Most states now use TANF rules in place of SNAP vehicle rules if the TANF rules are more beneficial to the SNAP household.

Most households also must meet an income limit. Certain things do not count as income and can be subtracted from your income. (Policy Advisory, USDHHR, 2013)

Creating cash support programs subsequent to those begun with the original Social Security Act, and repeated tinkering with the original cash support programs represent efforts to accommodate new social welfare demands without reshaping their foundation. The Social Security Act's cash support programs were predicated on benefits established through work in an economic world of individualism in which an inability to work was a personal matter. But as Chapter 3 shows beneficiary groups were added and benefits were changed to accommodate subtle changes in individual workforce participation. In addition, the advent of macroeconomic activity has led to fiscal policies that have produced unprecedented national economic growth without accommodation to the changes in the nature of work these policies have perpetuated or to the erosion of economic individualism. Adjustments to American capitalism have saddled a traditional social welfare system with problems beyond its capacity to protect individuals from events such as the Great Recession or the more gradual social changes that perpetuate poverty.

The penchant to isolate Social Security from larger economic considerations exemplifies the problem of separating social welfare from economic decisions and developments. President Johnson included Social Security, which had been kept "off the budget" for years by Representative Wilbur

Mills, in his 1968 budget as an online item in order to minimize attention to the growing federal debt. Then, for the 1974 budget process, Congress approved the use of a "unified" budget by including the value of Social Security Trust Funds subjecting Social Security income and expenditures to the Congressional review process, rather than treating it as a closed decision of the Ways and Means Committee. In 1985, when Congress accepted the controversial recommendations of the Greenspan Commission, it took Social Security off the budget. Accounting for Social Security taxing, spending, and its reserves has bounced back and forth: off-budget from 1935 to 1968, on-budget from 1969 to 1985, off-budget from 1986 to 1990—for all purposes except computing the deficit—and off-budget for all purposes since 1990.[12] Whether Social Security is or is not part of the unified budget does not change its macroeconomic consequences however. Social Security expenditures and its source of funding are clearly fiscal policy issues, yet its programs are restrained by individualist thinking. Thus, from today's fiscal perspective, the payroll tax is an inferior method for funding a massive Social Security program, but the rhetoric of nineteenth-century economic individualism secures its political value.[13]

It is unclear how revised fiscal policy could facilitate social welfare development, but from a contemporary social welfare perspective effective public policy would suggest that today's social welfare commitments be reformed with a revised structural foundation. Harmonizing the existing cash assistance programs under a single administrative authority focused more pointedly at the needs of those with low income and people in poverty creates part of a modern social welfare foundation for America. This step would necessitate an integration of the different funding authorities these present cash support programs presently enjoy. While such an effort may be politically difficult at best, such a design asks for review in light of the inability to restrain poverty, in spite of various program expansions over the years. The build-up to the latest welfare reform in 1996 attempted to put several cash support programs into a single package but quickly ran into opposition from existing administrative agencies, which drew their authority from these separate programs, and the outside interest groups aligned with administrative interests that pressured for support of existing administrative authorities. This was particularly true of the Department of Agriculture, as noted in Chapter 5.

The present discussion proposes to harmonize the cash support programs outlined in the Introduction (Figure I.1) with the authority of the social insurances as presently provided under the Social Security Act. Such an adjustment to the cash support commitments of American social welfare, while difficult to implement, would recreate the structural base of American social welfare aligned with the challenges of the twenty-first century and reflect a pragmatic link with a new economic order called for by the recognition of America's economic failures that triggered the Great Recession. Such realignment recognizes the changed relationship between work and social welfare without sacrificing a commitment to full employment. As presently constituted when work disappears both the economic and social welfare systems fail. A new alignment would recognize the one to support the other as supposed by the Employment Act (see Figure 6.1).

A new foundation for America's social welfare structure must also recognize the shortcoming of a social welfare system of individual benefits based on dedicated individual earnings and acknowledge that the present system of providing a significant quantity of cash support now provided under the Social Security Act cannot be sustained under its present financing arrangement. A new social welfare structure would rely on the Constitutionality of the social insurance cash support programs now being provided under the authority of the Social Security Act that have been fully evaluated. On the other hand, those cash assistance services, particularly those dependent on the use of the grant-in-aid to states for welfare purposes, have recently encountered additional legal problems that add to the political issues they have always struggled with.[14]

The Social Security Administration has demonstrated its capacity to integrate existing cash support undertakings and to administer a unified cash support system. This agency has grown into the largest administrative agency of the federal government (not counting the men and women in military uniform). It operates 10 regional offices, 54 area offices, 1297 local field offices, 33 teleservice centers, and 156 hearing offices. It employs 68,833 full- and part-time workers who service 47 million claims a year among other duties. In spite of its size, the Social Security Administration is also one of the most effective and efficient of all federal administrative agencies. It manages the two largest cash income maintenance programs in the United States: Social Security and Supplemental Security Income. It operates with an administrative error rate in the OASI and the DI programs of about 1.6 percent; its administrative expenses in the OASI and DI programs are 0.9 percent. Among its other program administrative obligations, it also is responsible for some of the most comprehensive long-range actuarial studies in all of government and produces extensive social welfare research much of which focuses on the plight of low-income poverty populations. The Social Security Administration is *not* an error-prone, inefficient, ineffective, bureaucratic government agency.

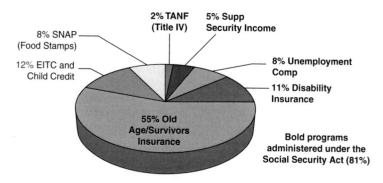

Figure 6.1   Federal cash support outlays

Source: Congressional Budget Office, 2013: Publications vary.

A TWENTY-FIRST-CENTURY CASH SUPPORT SOCIAL WELFARE PARADIGM

The Social Insurances

Rebuilding the foundation for America's cash support commitments begins with the social insurances as the most promising course to reflect the realities of America's twenty-first-century social welfare needs: mitigating poverty while improving the social welfare structure.

Social Security: There are two documents developed during the recent concern for the federal debt that rise above political posturing and provide a thoughtful beginning for restructuring Social Security, to allow it to become more effective in the battle against poverty: the President's Deficit Commission Report,[15] co-chaired by former Senator Alan Simpson and Erskine Bowles,[16] and the report of the Bipartisan Policy Center,[17] co-chaired by Pete Domenici and Alice Rivlin.[18] Although neither report has attracted political support, both reports take similar positions on Social Security, suggesting a more effective future course.

"Simpson/Bowles" began with a set of guiding principles including protecting the disadvantaged with Social Security benefits focused on those who need them the most.[19] The Domenici/Rivlin report begins assuming the importance of recovering from the recession and taking "steps to reduce the unsustainable debt that will be driven by the aging of the population, the rapid growth of health care costs, exploding interest costs, and the failure of policymakers to limit and prioritize spending."[20] The

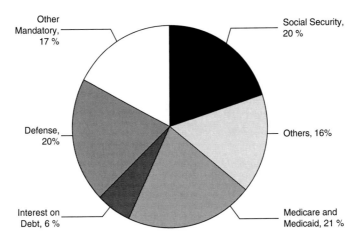

Figure 6.2   Relative weight of Social Security spending
Source: Bureau of the Budget, The White House, 2013.

disturbing feature of both of these reports is summarized by the Bipartisan Fiscal Commission report, which identifies the large share of spending on programs funded under the authority of the Social Security Act (see Figure 6.2). Any significant changes to Social Security will have to face the large share of public spending already allocated to it.

Social Security benefits: Both Domenici/Rivlin and Simpson/Bowles suggest Social Security changes that will reduce selected benefits in the longer term. Simpson/Bowles suggests a reconfiguration of benefits by recommending a Social Security minimum payment at the poverty level, which according to the Congressional Budget Office would raise Social Security outlays only by 0.1 percent, certainly a small amount.[21] Such a move would find favor with the thesis of the above discussions and would immediately reduce poverty in the SSI program by ensuring people with dual coverage would receive Social Security at the poverty level, and thus no longer need SSI.[22] Domenici/Rivlin would "Increase the minimum benefit for long-term, lower wage earners, and protect the most vulnerable elderly with a modest benefit increase."[23] Both reports recommend adjustments to benefit guarantees for higher earning retirees in order to increase long-range solvency and to accommodate improved benefits for lower earning retirees. Thus the reductions in Social Security spending would come at the expense of making Social Security more redistributive. For example, the Simpson/Bowles report recommends, "Modify the current three-bracket formula to a more progressive four bracket formula, with changes phased in slowly."[24] Domenici/Rivlin recommends, "Slightly reduce the growth in benefits compared to current law for approximately the top 25 percent of beneficiaries."[25] The Simpson/Bowles recommendations would expand the poverty-reducing capacity of Social Security in other ways as well (see Appendix 6.1).[26]

Financing Social Security: Chapter 3 outlines the unsteady development of Social Security, and its perennial issues of financing floats to the top of debates over its future for two reasons: Social Security spends large sums of money, and its long-range solvency is no longer viable under present financing arrangements. In the past, Social Security solvency has been secured by adjustments to the payroll tax, but further upward adjustments will be challenging, to say the least, particularly if new beneficiary groups are added or the basic level of benefits is increased as suggested below. The established combined payroll tax rate of 15.3 percent, half paid by employers and half paid by employees (including OASI, DI, and HI) may well be unsustainable at that level or beyond. Removing the cap on taxable income as recommended by both Domenici/Rivlin and Simpson/Bowles would relieve pressure in the short run, but like the many temporary financial fixes, this adjustment simply pushes the issue of the payroll tax down the road, a solution too often applied to Social Security financing. The larger the payroll tax rate grows the more regressive it becomes. Any payroll tax financing reprieve for Social Security is likely to be temporary. The payroll tax is a huge source of federal revenue, burdening workers most heavily (see Figure 6.3).

The payroll tax raises a politically charged financing issue. President Obama's 2 percent payroll tax holiday for employees and agreed to by Congress expired at the end of 2012, reminded Americans that macroeconomic decisions have important consequences for Social Security financing. In the 2012 case the Social Security Trust Fund was reimbursed by general revenue funds, a decided change in the way Social Security funding was dealt with in the past when trust fund income did not keep up with scheduled increases. Today payroll taxes raise almost as much revenue as do the general revenue taxes, and while these taxes are tightly locked for Social Security and Medicare spending, the income to their respective trust funds has been allowed to fluctuate, mostly for macroeconomic reasons. Although the payroll taxes collected to support Social Security cannot be used to fund other programs, general revenue taxes are now co-mingled with payroll taxes to support Social Security, which was the decision in 2012 (see Figure 6.4).

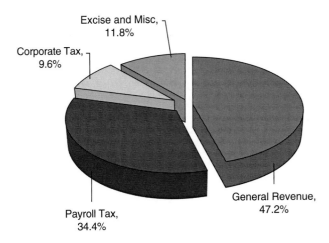

Figure 6.3   Source of Federal revenue, 2013

Source: Bureau of the Budget, The White House, 2013.

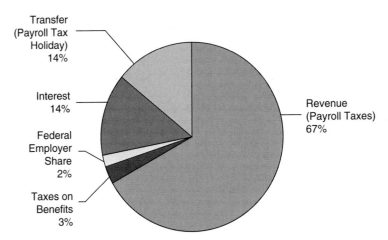

Figure 6.4   Sources of income to OAI and DI Social Security trust funds total income, 2012

Source: Congressional Budget Office, 2012.

General revenue funding for Social Security frequently has been discussed, and informally, and sometimes formally, has taken place. Any effort to modify Social Security's beneficiary base must consider a gradual replacement of the payroll tax with general revenue financing. Such a change would certainly be necessary if Supplemental Security Income were rolled into Social Security, as recommended below, since general revenue presently supports the SSI program. An increase in general revenue funding for Social Security, combined with a gradual decrease in the payroll tax, represents a prudent macroeconomic decision just as earlier Keynesian decisions changed the original way Social Security was funded to the twentieth-century.

Changing Social Security's revenue stream would likely provoke a full examination of its failing twentieth-century roots. For those who want to protect it, a complex battle over financing will force clarification of the twenty-first-century relationship between work and economic security. Thus, any effort to change the structure of Social Security financing would pull all the issues of Social Security into a debate. In other words it is difficult to envision changes to the payroll tax as a single tax issue. Considering the discussion about tax reform by both debt commissions, it is unlikely that forms of Social Security, despite its mandatory immunity, will remain exempt from future political debates anyway. Figure 6.4 shows the relative weight of Social Security spending and the big change it would take to replace payroll taxes with general revenue funds.

Unemployment Insurance: It might be difficult, but unemployment insurance must be wrestled from the Department of Labor and reformulated in the Social Security Administration where it began. Of all the economic and social revelations brought about by the present economic recession, perhaps none is more striking than the failure of unemployment insurance to meet the economic needs of people forced out of the work economy over the past five years. Built on the unemployment insurance structure created by the labor economists at the University of Wisconsin in 1935, Title III of the Social Security Act has shown the greatest inadequacy of all the cash support programs. Its outdated method of funding, its unevenness in administration across the states, and most significantly, its inability to lessen the impact of poverty on previously employed people combine to make unemployment insurance a prime candidate for inclusion under the Social Security Administration umbrella. In a situation of excessive and enduring unemployment, unemployment insurance is still geared to putting the unemployed back to work, when admittedly the economy has encountered massive job losses. In the present-day economic context, cash support for the unemployed must be separated from its back-to-work foundation in order to provide the economic security American workers should be able to receive.

The original Wisconsin model for unemployment insurance rested on the assumption that each industry/employer should be responsible for its own unemployment, justifying experience ratings and permitting wide state-to-state variations in program benefits. Thus, from 1935 to the present time this individually focused, "good business" orientation contrasted with a "worker protection" foundation for unemployment insurance under Title III. In addition there were concerns that a federally administered program might enhance the growing power of organized labor, and allow employees to dominate their employers, as the Wagner Act, which preceded the Social Security Act, seemed to have done.[27] These considerations led to the present form of unemployment insurance, which is characterized by time-limited benefits, an emphasis on getting people back to work, the tax-offset means of financing that favors employers, and administration under wide-ranging state rules for eligibility and benefit level. Job mobility in today's economy alone makes these criteria for unemployment insurance obsolete.

"Experience-based" unemployment insurance fails completely under circumstances like the present ones—when macroeconomic developments, rather than the practices of individual businesses, force high levels of unemployment that is neither the fault of the industry/employers or the workers themselves. The frequent need for special legislation to extend the unemployment benefit period, all paid directly by the federal government. Clearly, the inadequate amount of unemployment benefits all attest to the failure of this program to secure economic security for workers. For example the average worker benefit during the Great Recession (2011–12) was $303.87 per week, 82 percent of the poverty level for a three-person family and 68 percent of the poverty line for a family of four. Weekly benefits ranged from a high of $398.65 in Massachusetts to a low of $194.55 in Mississippi. While employed, most unemployed were gaining Social Security credits that stopped when they lost their jobs. Unemployment insurance was created as social insurance, and like Social Security, promoted as an "earned entitlement" even though its entitlement legitimacy is highly questionable. Moreover, unemployment insurance has been assigned a very small role in today's Department of Labor, which emphasizes employment. Of the over 3 million unemployed workers who presently receive unemployment benefits, about half that many remain unemployed but have exhausted their benefits. Unemployment insurance just does not work well on behalf of the worker.

Bringing unemployment insurance back to the Social Security Administration will allow Unemployment Insurance to set a poverty-level benefit and provide uniform administration across the states. Since the federal government essentially pays all of the costs of the insurance benefits, standard eligibility criteria would obviate the need for "experience-based" program funding and reduce the influence employers presently exert on state officials to keep their obligations to the unemployed as minimum as possible. Since a modernized Social Security program will continue to base its benefits to some extent on earnings, Unemployment Insurance under a changed administration would also integrate information of all types of work-related benefits into the Social Security information bank for later use determining eligibility. Such integration would not eliminate separate beneficiary rules for unemployment insurance, but would bring them into closer harmony with Social Security.

The Cash Assistance Programs

With a solid financial footing and with a guaranteed poverty-level benefit, a renovated Social Security program will have the capacity to bring existing cash assistance programs administered under the Social Security Act under its umbrella. A twenty-first-century Social Security program will lift the poverty burden of those presently receiving Supplemental Security Income, and extend financial support to economically dependent children who presently find financial support under the Temporary Assistance to Needy Families. This proposal simply recognizes the unfinished agenda proposed by various income maintenance options that gave rise to the Supplemental Security Income program in the first place, and solidifies a modest income base for most people in poverty.

Supplemental Security Income (SSI): The 2014 average monthly SSI payment is $535.00 per month, 55 percent of the poverty line for a single person and 41 percent of the poverty level for a two-person family. This national average includes the amount that individual states may provide to supplement SSI, an individual state option that only about one-half of the states exercise. All of the 8 million SSI recipients are in poverty. Establishing a poverty line minimum for Social Security beneficiaries would automatically remove about 2 million SSI recipients who receive both Social Security and SSI at the same time. Blending the remaining approximately 6 million SSI recipients into Social Security at the poverty level could cost an additional $2 billion, according to present spending patterns.

Temporary Assistance to Needy Families (TANF): Today more than 15 million children live in poverty (see Figure I.1), but only a scant

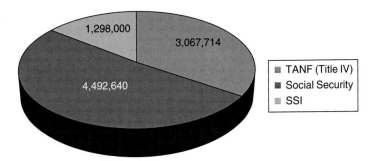

Figure 6.5   Number of poor children receiving cash support by program type
Source: TANF Tenth Annual Report to Congress.

3 million are receiving financial assistance under Temporary Assistance to Needy Families (TANF). The levels of assistance children now receive borders on criminal: an average of $355.40 per month, amounting to 38 percent of the poverty level. Since a large number of children receive either Social Security or SSI, bumping the benefits levels of these two programs up to the poverty level would leave approximately 3 million children dependent on cash support assistance from TANF. Unfortunately, TANF assistance uses only 28 percent of its funding for direct cash support, lessening cash relief even further for otherwise financially dependent children. As a result, the cash support to children who live under TANF is the lowest of any of the existing cash support programs. This is consistent with a recent study by the Brookings Institution and the Urban Institute that found "for every dollar spent on low-income children, 68 cents is on in kind benefits, 19 cents on refundable tax credits, 8 cents on monthly cash benefits, and 6 cents on reductions in tax liabilities.... These analyses reveal that the federal government uses in-kind spending as a primary way to deliver benefits and services to low-income children."[28] Children must be brought more fully into Social Security's income maintenance home (see Figure 6.5). Figure 6.5 shows how poor children receiving cash support are scattered throughout different programs.

Earned Income Tax Credit (EITC) and Supplemental Nutrition Assistance Program (SNAP): Because these programs are not easily understood as income maintenance programs, it is difficult to integrate them into a unified social welfare framework under Social Security as proposed in this chapter. Yet as hybrid cash programs that do reduce poverty, they need a similar twenty-first-century base in order to continue and improve their effectiveness. It is possible to suggest how both can be brought into harmony with the expanded capacity of Social Security.

Earned Income Tax Credit (EITC): EITC perhaps represents the best contemporary example of shaping social welfare responses to shortcomings in America's economic system rather than first correcting the system's economic deficiencies. It is difficult to explain why America's highly acclaimed capitalism cannot create enough jobs to provide employment at above-poverty wages, and thus requires government subsidies to low-paid workers. EITC not only subsidizes low-income workers, it also indirectly subsidizes employers who are able to profit from low-wage employment. EITC clearly rests on pre-twenty-first-century ideas that there is always some work, and that any work is economically better than no work. This point of view requires government to pay people to work. A Keynesian viewpoint might agree with this historic line of thinking as a way to promote a full employment economy. However, it might also argue that resources used to make sure people work are used for public purposes, not to enhance private enterprise. Simply put, if the private sector cannot provide enough jobs with above poverty wages, then the government must. Even with the present EITC program, the private sector cannot create enough jobs for all who need them. It seems prudent, therefore, to rethink EITC in light of the need to reconsider how America manages its economy in light of the Great Recession and the present halting recovery from it.

Called "work incentives," Social Security presently allows for limited earnings without jeopardizing its benefits. Special rules make it possible for people with disabilities receiving either Social Security or Supplemental Security Income (SSI) to work and still receive monthly payments, as well as Medicare or Medicaid coverage and other program benefits. These are existing work incentives that can be adopted to the cash supplements now provided through EITC.[29] Since most recipients of EITC would qualify for SSI if EITC were placed under a new authority in the Social Security Administration, it would be possible to include a special class of people under SSI recipients—made up of those presently receiving EITC benefits. This would leave the tax treatment of these low-income workers with the Treasury Department, but relieve it of sending cash supplements to them. It would also assure low-income workers of the social benefits extended to SSI recipients, such as Medicaid.

Supplemental Nutrition Assistance Program (SNAP): SNAP presents special political problems for blending its resources under a revised Social Security format of the type noted above. Since SNAP now uses electronic debit cards in place of stamps, the transition to a supplemental program under Social Security would be easy if the political problems could be overcome.

CONCLUSION

Our present social welfare system failed under the stress of the Great Recession, and calls for a changed economic system, such leading economists have made, are also appeals for a changed social welfare system. The failure of America's social welfare programs to protect Americans from the personal destruction of the system-wide economic collapse provided an unvarnished view of the inadequacy of our social welfare commitments to reduce poverty over the past 50 years. America's present social welfare system, with the social insurances at the center, was founded on eighteenth- and nineteenth-century economic and social principles, which have little ability to anchor twenty-first-century American commitments. The Great Recession exposed the structural flaws these principles have created in today's economic and social welfare systems. Unfortunately, macroeconomic planning (a product of the Employment Act of 1946) has produced fiscal policies that have not always been friendly to American social welfare. For example, there is ample evidence to support the argument that Keynesian economics laid the groundwork for present-day Social Security economic crises. Had the Social Security Trust Fund(s) been allowed to grow as Roosevelt first demanded, and if the addition of new beneficiaries required additional funding (as in the case of creating Disability Insurance), the Social Security and Disability Trust Funds today would be bulging, something American capitalism, as we knew it, could not tolerate. The fiscal policies necessary to preserve American capitalism literally short-changed the long-term value of our social insurances.

There are also larger fiscal policies like trading inflation control with unemployment, without appropriate compensation for the individuals who suffer the unemployment. Other fiscal policies that have allowed income inequality to grow have shown little regard for their social welfare consequences, such as America's perpetual poverty. Thus while macroeconomic activities have moved American capitalism well beyond its eighteenth- and nineteenth-century origins, social welfare remains tethered to the past.

The non-cash social welfare programs America has created are not really anti-poverty programs but spending that allows low-income people to obtain a certain amount of parity with the rest of the population, a contention validated by the Supplemental Poverty Measure, as explained in

Chapter 2. Today's cash support programs peg their minimum payments well below any poverty targets, with the exception of Social Security, particularly for the aged. Melding the cash support programs under a single administrative authority and integrating them with the changing environment of work, while not all that novel, would involve some important changes, beginning with consolidation of the cash support programs under the authority of Social Security, the anchor of American social welfare. This would require moving away from the payroll tax to general revenue. It would also require moving unemployment insurance from the Labor Department back to the Social Security Administration and integrating the cash transfer of EITC under a revised Supplemental Security Income program. While there may be little confidence such changes could be politically possible, it seems important to generate ideas that will move the nation's social welfare enterprise into the present century. It appears timely that something like the Hoover Commission is needed to develop detailed recommendations and specific structural changes based on the comprehensive social welfare restructuring suggested in this chapter. Similar to the Hoover Commission, which had a profound effect on reshaping our government after World War Two, a similar social welfare commission would shape our government social welfare commitments into the new forms required by twenty-first-century global economic considerations.

Joseph Stiglitz writes,

> It may be true that 'the poor always ye have with you,' but that doesn't mean that there have to be *so many* poor, or that they should suffer so much. We have the wealth and resources to eliminate poverty: Social Security and Medicare have almost eliminated poverty among the elderly. And other countries, not as rich as the United States, have done a better job of reducing poverty and inequality.
>
> It is particularly disturbing that today almost a quarter of all children live in poverty. Not doing anything about their plight is a political choice that will have long-lasting consequences for our country. [30]

For America, inequality and poverty are a political choice. The Great Recession allows a retrospective of social welfare and the political development of the American economy, and to the extent that economists urge a reconstructed American economy, a reconstructed social welfare enterprise also cries for building. Simply to continue social welfare drift is unacceptable to the millions of Americans dependent on existing programs, and it will not further the success of the American enterprise in the years to come.

The economic reforms, which are presently debated, not only must consider protecting the economy from another economic disaster, but they also must envision corresponding social welfare improvements that will reduce poverty and provide economic security for those caught in recurring structural economic adjustments. America presently spends substantial amounts of its Gross National Product for social welfare purposes, mostly under the authority of the Social Security Act. America has an effective social welfare structure in place. The Social Security Administration is capable of joining the cash assistance programs to assure that America is able to respond to her twenty-first century challenges.

Appendix I.1 America's Cash Support Commitments[a]

	Social Security—Old Age and Survivors Disability and Health Insurance (OASDHI Title II of the Act) $774,825 Million[a]
	Old Age Insurance (The Act, Title II, 1935) Cash to retirees, spouses, and their children (Chapter 2)
	Disability Insurance (The Act Title II, 1954) Cash to disabled who qualify (Chapter 2)
The Social Security Act	Hospital Insurance (The Act Title XVIII, 1965) Noncash benefits Part A—In-hospital care Part B—Outpatient care Part D—Drug Insurance
	Unemployment Insurance/Compensation (Title III of the Act) Cash to qualifying unemployed persons
	Supplemental Security Income (Title XIV of the Act) Cash to Low-Income Aged and Disabled
	Temporary Assistance to Needy Families (Title IV of the Act) Cash to low-income families with children
Earned Income Tax Credit	EITC reduces the federal tax of low-income workers to zero and any leftover credit is refunded to the worker in cash if the worker's income is below the filing requirement. Tax credit, and direct cash.
Supplemental Nutrition Assistance Program	SNAP provides financial support for food purchases for low-income families through the use of an electronic benefit card which can be used for buying specific foods from specified vendors. It does not distribute cash directly.

^aThe OASDI program provided benefit payments to more than about 57 million people: 40 million retired workers and dependents of retired workers, 6 million survivors of deceased workers, and 11 million disabled workers and their dependents.

8,295,013 persons received SSI payments amounting to a total of $4,612,279,000 for an average payment of $526.41 in 2013.

TANF reported 3,916,077 average cases for FY 2013, of which 2,917,397 were children. Expenditures to states totaled $16,488,667,000. Nationwide in 2012, over 27 million received nearly $62 billion in EITC for the 2011 tax year.

In the 2012 fiscal year, $74.6 billion in food assistance was distributed to 47.7 million persons for an average $134.29 per month in food assistance.

Appendix 1.1   Number and Percent of People in Poverty by Different Poverty Measures: 2010 ❧

Characteristic	**Number (in thousands)	Official**				SPM				Difference	
		Number		Percent		Number		Percent		Number	Percent
		Est.	90 percent C.I.¹ (±)	Est.	90 percent C.I.¹ (±)	Est.	90 percent C.I.¹ (±)	Est.	90 percent C.I.¹ (±)		
All People	306,110	46,602	850	15.2	0.3	49,094	908	16.0	0.3	*2,492	*0.8
Age											
Under 18 years	74,916	16,823	378	22.5	0.5	13,622	376	18.2	0.5	*_3,201	*_4.3
18 to 64 years	192,015	26,258	556	13.7	0.3	29,235	602	15.2	0.3	*2,976	*1.6
65 years and older	39,179	3,520	161	9.0	0.4	6,237	216	15.9	0.6	*2,716	*6.9
Type of Unit											
In married couple unit	185,723	14,200	581	7.6	0.3	18,295	622	9.9	0.3	*4,095	*2.2
In female householder unit	61,966	17,786	513	28.7	0.7	17,991	552	29.0	0.8	206	0.3
In male householder unit	32,224	5,927	289	18.4	0.8	7,317	308	22.7	0.8	*1,391	*4.3
In new SPM unit	26,197	8,690	341	33.2	1.0	5,490	339	21.0	1.2	*_3,200	*_12.2
Race and Hispanic Origin											
White	243,323	31,959	698	13.1	0.3	34,747	728	14.3	0.3	*2,789	*1.1
White, not Hispanic	197,423	19,819	571	10.0	0.3	21,876	605	11.1	0.3	*2,057	*1.0
Black	39,031	10,741	406	27.5	1.0	9,932	388	25.4	1.0	*_810	*_2.1
Asian	14,332	1,737	161	12.1	1.1	2,397	191	16.7	1.3	*660	*4.6
Hispanic (any race)	49,972	13,346	420	26.7	0.8	14,088	459	28.2	0.9	*742	*1.5
Nativity											
Native born	267,884	38,965	801	14.5	0.3	39,329	845	14.7	0.3	364	0.1
Foreign born	38,226	7,636	288	20.0	0.7	9,765	327	25.5	0.7	*2,128	*5.6
Naturalized citizen	16,801	1,910	119	11.4	0.7	2,829	158	16.8	0.9	*919	*5.5
Not a citizen	21,424	5,727	263	26.7	1.1	6,936	288	32.4	1.2	*1,209	*5.6

Tenure											
Owner	207,290	16,529	565	8.0	0.3	20,205	659	9.7	0.3	*3,676	*1.8
Owner/mortgage	138,324	8,366	389	6.0	0.3	11,419	471	8.3	0.3	*3,053	*2.2
Owner/no mortgage/ rent-free	72,180	9,036	413	12.5	0.5	9,581	429	13.3	0.6	*544	*0.8
Renter	95,606	29,199	740	30.5	0.6	28,093	746	29.4	0.6	_1,106	_1.2
Residence											
Inside MSAs	258,350	38,650	932	15.0	0.3	42,979	879	16.6	0.3	*4,329	*1.7
Inside principal cities	98,774	19,584	585	19.8	0.5	20,748	611	21.0	0.6	*1,164	*1.2
Outside principal cities	159,576	19,066	742	11.9	0.4	22,231	738	13.9	0.4	*3,165	*2.0
Outside MSAs	47,760	7,951	544	16.6	0.7	6,114	449	12.8	0.7	_1,837	_3.8
Region											
Northeast	54,782	7,051	327	12.9	0.6	7,969	342	14.5	0.6	*918	*1.7
Midwest	66,104	9,246	410	14.0	0.6	8,678	356	13.1	0.5	_569	_0.9
South	113,275	19,210	577	17.0	0.5	18,503	533	16.3	0.5	_707	_0.6
West	71,949	11,094	447	15.4	0.6	13,944	512	19.4	0.7	*2,849	*4.0
Health Insurance Coverage											
With private insurance	195,874	9,336	360	4.8	0.2	14,631	464	7.5	0.2	*5,295	*2.7
With public, no private insurance	60,332	22,694	600	37.6	0.8	19,126	559	31.7	0.8	_3,568	_5.9
Not insured	49,904	14,571	408	29.2	0.7	15,337	474	30.7	0.8	*766	*1.5

* Statistically different from zero at the 90 percent confidence level.

** Differs from published official rates as unrelated individuals under 15 years of age are included in the universe.

1 Confidence Interval obtained using replicate weights (Fay's Method). Note: Details may not sum to totals because of rounding.

Source: U.S. Census Bureau, Current Population Survey, 2011 Annual Social and Economic Supplement.

Appendix 3.1   Changes in Social Security Beneficiaries: 1935–81 ❧

Year	Beneficiary	Year	Beneficiary
1935	Retired worker aged 65 and over	1961	Retired man aged 62–64 Husband aged 62–64 Dependent widower aged 62 and over Dependent male parent aged 62–64 Full-time student aged 18–21
1939	Wife aged 65 and over Child under age 18 Widowed mother any age caring for eligible child Widow aged 65 and over Dependent parent aged 65 and over	1965	Widow aged 60–61 Full-time student aged 18–21 Divorced wife age 62 and over Divorced wife aged 60 and over
		1967	Disabled widow aged 50–59 Disabled widower aged 50–61
1950	Wife under age 65 caring for eligible child Husband aged 65 and over Dependent widower aged 65 and over	1972	Disabled widower aged 50–59
1956	Dependent female parent aged 62–64 Retired woman aged 62–64 Disabled worker aged 50–64 Wife aged 62–64 Disabled child age 18 and over Widow aged 62–64 Disabled child aged 18 and over	1975	Widowed father caring for eligible child
		1976	Divorced husband aged 62 and over
		1978	Husband under age 65 caring for eligible child
1958	Same as dependents of retired recipient Disabled worker under age 65	1981	Student category eliminated, except for high school students under age 19

Source: Geoffrey Kollmann, "Social Security: Summary of Major Changes in the Cash Benefits Program," Washington, DC: Congressional Research Service, May, 2000.

Appendix 6.1   Highlights of the Simpson/Bowles Recommendations on Social Security ✧

- Gradually increase taxable maximum income to cover 90% of earnings by 2050.
- Apply refined cost of living measure (chained-CPI) to COLA.
- Gradually phase in progressive changes to the benefit formula thus lessening benefits for high earning Social Security beneficiaries.
- Offer a minimum benefit of 125% of poverty for an individual with 25 years of work.
- Create "hardship exemption" for those unable to work.
- Provide benefit enhancement equal to 5% of the average benefits for individuals who have been eligible for benefits for 20 years.
- Add increased flexibility in retirement claiming options.

Source: *The Moment of Truth: Report of the National Commission on Fiscal Responsibility and Reform*, Washington, DC: The White House, December 1, 2010.

Notes ✑

PREFACE

1. Harold Wilensky and Charles Lebeaux, *Industrial Society and Social Welfare* (New York: Russell Sage Foundation, 1958), p. 138, note 1.

INTRODUCTION

1. *Webster's New Collegiate Dictionary* (Springfield, MA: G. & C. Merriam, 1977), p. 1065.
2. The Townsend Plan boasted of 5,000 Townsend clubs across the nation with more than 5 million members. During work on the Social Security Act, Townsend presented President Roosevelt a petition with more than 20,000 signatures supporting the Townsend plan.
3. *Catalog of Federal Domestic Assistance* (*CFDA*) provides a full listing of all federal programs available to state and local governments (including the District of Columbia); federally recognized Indian tribal governments; territories (and possessions) of the United States; domestic public, quasi-public, and private profit and nonprofit organizations and institutions; specialized groups; and individuals. See www.cfda.gov
4. This mandate and its constitutionality are discussed in the next chapter.

1   POVERTY'S ELUSIVE HEREDITY

1. John Kenneth Galbraith, *The Affluent Society* (Boston: Houghton Mifflin, 1958), p. 313.
2. George Gilder, *Wealth and Poverty* (New York: Basic Books, 1981), p. 111.
3. Amos Warner, *American Charities: A Study in Philanthropy and Economics* (New York: Crowell, 1894). See also Andrew Dobelstein, *Moral Authority, Ideology, and the Future of American Social Welfare* (Boulder, CO: Westview Press, 1999), pp. 219–20.
4. The significance of the social reform movement in the development of changing attitudes towards the poor is discussed at length in Dobelstein, *Moral Authority.*

5. James T. Patterson, *America's Struggle against Poverty in the Twentieth Century* (4e) (Cambridge, MA: Harvard University Press, 2000).

6. *Proceedings of the Conference on the Care of Dependent Children* (Washington, DC: Government Printing Office, 1909), p. 224.

7. The other two reasons for dependency were children who were deserted by their parents and children from inadequate homes who had to be removed for their own good. "This aid should be given by such methods and form such sources as may be determined by the general relief policy of each community preferably in the form of private charity, rather than public relief" (ibid., p. 10).

8. A further discussion in Chapter 4 argues that the focus of the Children's Bureau began to shift away from the economic welfare of children in the late 1980s as its influence diminished during the 1990 debates on welfare reform. The Children's Bureau was initially placed in the Department of Labor.

9. Andrew Dobelstein, *Serving Older Adults* (Prentice Hall: Englewood Cliffs, 1985), particularly pp. 68–75 and 119–25.

10. See Andrew Dobelstein, *Moral Authority and the Future of American Social Welfare* (Boulder, CO: Westview Press, 1999), pp. 92–104.

11. Michael Harrington, *The Other America* (New York: Macmillan, 1962), p. 6.

12. The Job Corps, Neighborhood Youth Corps, Work Study, Urban and Rural Community Action, Adult Basic Education, Voluntary Assistance for Needy Children, Loans to Rural Families, Assistance for Migrant Agricultural Employees, Employment and Investment Incentives, Work Experience and Training for AFDC mothers, and Volunteers in Service to America (VISTA) were created by the Economic Opportunity Act. None of these programs were designed to provide cash directly to the poor.

13. Wilbur Cohen distanced himself from the OEO and preferred to keep programs and spending within the Social Security Administration. "When you've got some completely new ideas, they will go farther and faster in a new agency than in an old agency.... What you're doing is, you're being experimental and innovative—which requires a somewhat different mentality and experience than an old-line fellow who can take something and make it work in a methodical way." Quoted in Michael L. Gillette, *Launching the War on Poverty. An Oral History* (New York: Twayne Publishers, 1996), p. 343.

14. Patterson, *America's Struggle against Poverty*, pp. 146–47.

15. Charles A. Murray, *Losing Ground: American Social Policy, 1950–1980* (New York: Basic Books, 1984).

16. See US Congress, House of Representatives, Committee on Ways and Means, *The Social Security Amendments of 1971* (Washington, DC: US Government Printing Office, 1971), p. 7. Daniel Moynihan complained that Johnson's efforts were hypocritical since the Heineman Commission did not make its report until President Johnson left office. He argued that Johnson so acted so as to leave a legacy that would be difficult for Nixon to fulfill. The Heineman

Commission's recommendations were well known before President Nixon presented his welfare proposals in 1969. See Daniel Moynihan, *The Politics of a Guarantee Income* (New York: Vintage Books, 1973), pp. 128–35. The report of the ways and means Committee cited differs from Moynihan's. See pp. 46–64.

17. See Milton Friedman, *Essays in Positive Economics* (Chicago: University of Chicago Press, 1962) and Milton Friedman, *Capitalism and Freedom* (Chicago: University of Chicago Press, 1962). Friedman supported a guaranteed income as a way to reduce government by providing a grant of income without government intervention into a "free market system" that attempted to regulate the "marketplace" in order to improve the economic welfare of the poor.

18. See also Robert Theobald, *The Guaranteed Income* (New York: Doubleday, 1965).

19. Legacies of the War on Poverty (National Poverty Series on Poverty and Public Policy) Hardcover by Martha J. Bailey (Author, Editor), Sheldon Danziger (Editor). This insightful volume refutes pessimism about the effects of social policies and provides new lessons about what more can be done to improve the lives of the poor.

20. Dobelstein, *Moral Authority*, pp. 30, 31.

21. Republicans who controlled the House of Representatives proposed to use their welfare reform to overthrow the New Deal programs. Ron Haskins, *Work over Welfare. The Inside Story of the 1996 Welfare Reform Law* (Washington, DC: Brookings Institution Press, 2006), p. 85. See also Andrew Dobelstein, *Understanding the Social Security Act* (New York: Oxford University Press, 2009), p. 200.

22. Gordon M. Fisher, *Reasons for Measuring Poverty in the United States in the Context of Public Policy—A Historical Review, 1916–1995* (Washington, DC: US Department of Health and Human Services, 1999), revised in June 2000.

23. "Poverty status is determined by comparing annual income to a set of dollar values called thresholds that vary by family size, number of children, and age of householder. If a family's before tax money income is less than the dollar value of their threshold, then that family and every individual in it are considered to be in poverty. For people not living in families, poverty status is determined by comparing the individual's income to his or her threshold" (US Census Bureau, American Community Survey, 2011).

24. Elise Gould and Hilary Wething, "U.S. Poverty Rates Higher, Safety Net Weaker Than in Peer Countries," Issue Brief # 339, Washington, DC, Economic Policy institute, July 24, 2012, pp. 2–4.

25. Kathleen S. Short, "The Supplemental Poverty Measure: Examining the Incidence and Depth of Poverty in the U.S. Taking Account of Taxes and Transfers in 2011," Washington, DC: US Census Bureau, 2012.

26. Gould and Wething, "U.S. Poverty Rates Higher," no page number.

27. Today the Children's Bureau is an organization within the Administration of Children, Youth and Families, one of eleven operating divisions (program agencies) reporting directly to the Secretary of the Department of Health and Human Services. Although it wields authority over the several federal programs designed specifically to assist children and youth, including TANF, its influence in decision-making is considerably less than it was in 1935. The federal government has delegated much of its research and advocacy on poverty issues to Institute for Poverty at the University of Wisconsin through a generous funding of its programs.

28. "The results [from the SPM] illustrate differences between the official measure of poverty and a poverty measure that takes account of in-kind benefits received by families and nondiscretionary expenses that they must pay. The SPM also employs a new poverty threshold that is updated with information on expenses for food, clothing, shelter, and utilities. Results showed higher poverty rates using the SPM than the official measure for most groups." Short, "Supplemental Poverty Measure," p. 21. Please see Appendix 1 of this chapter for a full report on the SPM, its development, and its use.

29. Lawrence, Mishel, Josh Bivens, Elise Gould, and Heidi Shierholz, "Poverty," in *The State of Working America*, 12th edn (Washington, DC: Cornell University Press, 2012).

30. Ibid., pp. 438–48.

31. Congressional Budget Office, "Trends in the Distribution of Household Income between 1979 and 2007," October 2011.

32. Paul Krugman has referred to efforts to correlate everything with desired results "statistical malpractice."

2 A NEW CAPITALIST ORDER NEEDS A NEW SOCIAL WELFARE MANDATE

1. The relative poverty rate is the share of individuals with incomes below half of household-size-adjusted median income. Poverty rates are based on income after taxes and transfers. The relative poverty rate is the most frequently used measure for international economic comparisons. See Chapter 1.

2. Lawrence Mishel, Josh Bivens, Elise Gould, and Heidi Shierholz, "Poverty," *The State of Working America* (12e) (Ithaca, NY: Cornell University Press, 2012), p. 449.

3. Joseph E. Stiglitz, *Freefall: America, Free Markets, and the Sinking of the World Economy* (New York: W. W. Norton, 2010), p. 187.

4. Sean Wilentz, *The Rise of American Democracy* (New York: W. W. Norton, 2005), p. xxi.

5. Robert Heilbroner was Professor of Economics at the New School for Social for more than 20 years. His book *Worldly Philosophers* (1953) has sold nearly

four million copies—the second-best-selling economics text of all time. The seventh edition was published in 1999.

6. Robert Heilbroner, "Reflections: The Triumph of Capitalism," *The New Yorker* (January 23, 1989), pp. 98–99.

7. Many political economists would prefer to use the words "market system" in place of the word capitalism to define America's present economic system.

8. This discussion uses http://www2.hn.psu.edu/faculty/jmanis/adam-smith/Wealth-Nations.pdf as the electronic version for source material in this chapter.

9. Adam Smith, *The Theory of Moral Sentiments* (London: A. Millar, 1759).

10. The allusion to an invisible hand comes well into Smith's discussion of labor exchanges and there is no reason to believe this concept had the same importance for Smith as it has had for contemporary neoconservative economists. The only specific mention of "invisible hand" in the Wealth of Nations that this author can identify appears on page 364 in the edition referenced in note number 8. It is, however, an important concept in Smith's *The Theory of Moral Sentiments*.

11. This discussion uses http://www2.hn.psu.edu/faculty/jmanis/adam-smith/Wealth-Nations.pdf as the electronic version for source material in this chapter.

12. Milton Friedman, *Capitalism and Freedom* (Chicago: University of Chicago Press, 1962).

13. Friedman, p. 13, italics in original.

14. Ibid., p. 9.

15. Ibid., p. 27.

16. John Hallowell notes, "It should be emphasized that the freedom of economic enterprise which Smith advocated was essentially *individual* economic enterprise. He would have tolerated few of the modern corporations which since his time have largely replaced individually owned and operated business." Smith's work is a plea for the economic freedom of the individual and a violent attack on economic systems that emerged from mercantilism according to Hallowell. John Hallowell, *Main Currents in Modern Political Thought* (New York: Holt, Rinehart and Winston, 1950), p. 140, italics in original.

17. John Locke, *Two Treatises of Government* (London: Black Swan, 1698), Book 2, chapter 5, p. 5. (Locke's title was "Two Treatises of Government: In the Former, the False Principles and Foundation of Sir Robert Filmer, and his Followers are Detected and Overthrown.") It is important to note that John Locke's establishment of private property reflected an idea of *productive* labor.

18. "The powers not delegated to the United States by the Constitution, nor prohibited by it to the States, are reserved to the States respectively, or to the people" (United States Constitution, Article X).

19. Montesquieu conceived the notion of divided government assigning separate powers into executive, legislative, and judicial functions, but Madison added the idea that the powers of one would check the power of the others: "checks and balances."

20. "The causes of faction cannot be removed, and... relief is only to be sought in the means of controlling its effects. If a faction consists of less than a majority, relief is supplied by the republican principle, which enables the majority to defeat its sinister views by regular vote. It may clog the administration, it may convulse the society; but it will be unable to execute and mask its violence under the forms of the Constitution" (Federalist # 10, p. 66).

21. James MacGregor Burns, *The Deadlock of Democracy. Four Party Politics in America* (Englewood Cliffs, NJ: Prentice-Hall, 1963).

22. Max Weber, *The Protestant Ethic and the Spirit of Capitalism*, translated by Talcott Parsons, with a Foreword by R. H. Tawney (New York: Charles Scribner's Sons, 1958), p. 51, italics in original. Written in 1904–05, *The Protestant Ethic* did not appear in an English translation until 1930.

23. Quoted in Leonard Larabee, *The Papers of Benjamin Franklin*, vol. 4 (New Haven: Yale University Press, 1961), p. 480. See also Andrew Dobelstein, *Moral Authority, Ideology, and the Future of American Social Welfare* (Boulder, CO: Westview Press, 1999), chapter 7.

24. Weber, *The Protestant Ethic*, p. 167.

25. John Kenneth Galbraith summarized the neo-capitalist position this way: "Inequality came to be regarded as almost equally important for capital formation. Were income widely distributed, it would be spent. But if it flowed in a concentrated stream to the rich, a part would certainly be saved and invested." John Kenneth Galbraith, *The Affluent Society* (Boston: Houghton Mifflin, 1958), p. 79.

26. Joseph A. Schumpter, *Capitalism, Socialism, and Democracy* (New York: Harper and Brothers, 1950), p. 82.

27. Paul Krugman, Professor of Economics and International Affairs at Princeton University, and op. ed. contributor to *The New York Times*, won the Nobel Memorial Prize in Economic Sciences for his contributions to New Trade Theory in 2008. "Smart fiscal policy involves having the government spend when the private sector won't, supporting the economy when it is weak and reducing debt only when it is strong." Paul Krugman, "Dwindling Deficit Disorder," *New York Times*, March 11, 2013.

28. Paul Krugman, *The Return of Depression Economics and the Crisis of 2008* (New York: W. W. Norton, 2009), p. 30. John Kenneth Galbreath expressed a similar thought several years ago when he wrote, "The [current] economic system fabricated by Ricardo survived only because there was no evident alternative and certainly none that was better. Any effort to modify it made it less sufficient." *The Affluent Society*, p. 38.

29. The basic premises of American capitalism usually rest on freely operating markets, access to complete information, and no accommodation to the need

for public goods or consideration of economic externalities caused by market activity.

30. It is important to keep in mind that in 1854, President Franklyn Pierce vetoed legislation championed by Dorthea Dix designed to make public lands available for mental hospitals, clarifying the position of the federal government that prevailed until the Great Depression: "I can not find any authority in the Constitution for making the Federal Government the great almoner of public charity throughout the United States. To do so would, in my judgment, be contrary to the letter and spirit of the Constitution and subversive of the whole theory upon which the Union of these States is founded" (*Congressional Globe*, 33rd Congress, 1st Session, May 3, 1854. The Constitutionality of Social Security was affirmed in 1937 (see U.S. 633 at 640).

31. "The Committee on Economic Security that was charged with developing the Social Security Act (Originally called the Economic Security Act) was quite clear that any form of assistance was the responsibility of the states. "Public funds should be devoted to providing work rather than to introduce a relief element into what should be strictly an insurance program." Andrew Dobelstein, *Understanding the Social Security Act* (New York: Oxford University Press, 2009), p. 24.

32. "Those [social security] taxes were never a problem of economics. They are politics all the way through. We put those payroll contributions there so as to give the contributors a legal, moral and political right to collect their pensions and their unemployment benefits. With those taxes in there, no damn politician can ever scrap my social security program." President Franklin D. Roosevelt, 1935, quoted in William E. Leuchtenburg, *Franklin D. Roosevelt and the New Deal* (New York: Harper and Row, 1963), p. 133.

33. *General Theory of Employment, Interest and Money* (1936).

34. Paul Krugman, *Peddling Prosperity: Economic Sense and Nonsense in the Age of Diminished*, New York: W. W. Norton & Company, 1994. p. 51.

35. See *Full Employment in a Free Competitive Economy*, US Congress, Committee on Banking and Currency (79d Congress, 1st Session, 1945).

36. Steven Kemp Bailey, *Congress Makes a Law. The Story Behind the Employment Act of 1946* (New York: Columbia University Press, 1950).

37. Julian E. Zelizer, *Taxing America. Wilbur D. Mill, Congress, and the State, 1945–1975* (New York: Cambridge University Press, 1998), p. 15.

38. US Congress, Joint Economic Committee, *Studies in Welfare* (Washington, DC: Government Printing Office, 1972–74) (dates vary).

39. See Sheldon Danziger and Robert Haveman, *Understanding Poverty* (New York: Russell Sage Foundation, 2001). This 500-page volume of over 14 major research papers was a product of the highly influential institute for Research on Poverty at the University of Wisconsin-Madison, funded in part by the US Department of Health and Human services.

40. An old school economist, Secretary of the Treasury Morgenthau insisted that Social Security be economically sound "in perpetuity," and thus insisted on

large Social Security reserves. Morgenthau opposed Roosevelt's social spending. He commented once, "We have tried spending money. We are spending more than we have ever spent before and it does not work....After eight years of this administration we have just as much unemployment as when we started...and an enormous debt to boot!" John Morton Blum, *Roosevelt and Morgenthau* (Boston, MA: Houghton Mifflin Harcourt, 1970), p. 256. When Secretary Morgenthau informed President Roosevelt that Social Security income and expenditure projections showed shortfalls after the first 50 years, Roosevelt ordered his Committee on Economic Security to revise the projections before he presented the Social Security Act to Congress. See Dobelstein, *Understanding the Social Security Act*, p. 59.

41. Martha Derthick, *Policy Making for Social Security* (Washington, DC: Brookings Institution, 1979), p. 91.
42. Eric M. Patashnik, *Putting Trust in the US Budget* (New York: Cambridge University Press, 2000), p. 72.
43. In addition to its benefits to unemployed people, unemployment insurance provides an important example of Keynesian macroeconomic activity as a "countercyclical" or "automatic stabilizer" element in the national economy. As unemployment increases Unemployment Insurance puts money back into the economy, acting as an economic stabilizer, but such economic stimuli usually come at the expense of an increase in government debt, which, in the present case, Congress refused to expand. See Congressional Budget Office, *The Effects of Automatic Stabilizers on the Federal Budget as of 2013*, March, 2013.
44. Keynesian economics and the Employment Act argued that either increased government spending or reduced taxes would stimulate economic growth. According to Margaret Weir, the Council of Economic Advisors took the latter course in preference to the former in the development of fiscal policy. See Margaret Weir, "Federal Government and Unemployment," in Margaret Weir, Ann Shola Orloff, and Theda Skocpol (eds.), *The Politics of Social Policy in the United States* (Princeton, NJ: Princeton University Press, 1988), pp. 149–90.
45. Congress and the president have a long history of struggles over how to compromise macroeconomic authority with *laissez-faire* government associated with neoconservative capitalism. The focus of these struggles has usually been over government spending rather than on government income. Beginning in 1974, congress passed the Congressional Budget Act giving Congress more control over federal spending when President Nixon impounded nearly $12 billion of congressionally appropriated funds. In 1979, Paul Volker as Chairman of the Federal Reserve instituted a monetary policy in lieu of interest rate policy as a macroeconomic management tool to keep control on government spending. In 1985 and 1986, Congress created Graham-Rudman-Hollings and Graham-Rudman-Hollings II as a way to limit spending and established the process of "sequestration" if budget goals were not met. Several budgets by

the reconciliation process, a shutdown of the federal government in 1996, the American Recovery and Reinvestment Act of 2009, and the fiscal impasses of 2012 and 2013 all reflect the difficulty of blending various economic assumptions with increasing authority on the part of the federal government to regulate the economy as begun in 1946. See http://bancroft.berkeley.edu/ ROHO/projects/debt/americanrecoveryact.html for a clear summary of these events.

46. Stiglitz, *Freefall*, p. xxi.

47. Ibid., p. 198.

48. Social Security Administration, *Annual Statistical Supplement*, Washington, DC, 2012, Table 4.A1.

49. "Between 2005 and 2011, the number of households with children under 18 that had at least one unemployed parent rose by one-third (33%) across the United States. States experiencing a larger than average increase included Hawaii (95%), California (61%), Nevada (148%), and Colorado (56%) in the West and Florida (93%), North Carolina (54%), New Jersey (63%), and Connecticut (65%) in the East." US Census Bureau, *America's Families and Living Arrangements: 2012*. August, 2013, p. 28.

50. The US Department of Labor has published a comparison of state unemployment laws revealing that no two states have the same criteria for basic unemployment benefit eligibility, amount of weekly payments, and length of benefit eligibility (US Department of Labor, "Comparison of State Unemployment Laws," January 2012). DOL has also produced a summary of federal UI legislation that summarizes over 125 different statutory changes to this legislation since 1939 in its 108-page summary report. "Chronology of Federal Unemployment Compensation Laws for Informational Purposes," January, 2013.

51. The Social Security Administration is unable to estimate this number.

52. Public Law 111–312, the Tax Relief, Unemployment Insurance Reauthorization, and Job Creation Act of 2010.

53. The 2012 OASDI Trustees Report, Office of the Chief Actuary, Social Security Administration, 2013.

54. The Earned Income Tax Credit, while not an insurance program provides a tax credit to workers in low-paying jobs, but obviously if a person is not working there is no EITC.

55. Stiglitz, *Freefall*, p. xix.

3   THE SOCIAL INSURANCES

1. Present-day social welfare programs under the authority of the Social Security Act are Social Security, both Retirement, Survivors Insurance, and Disability Insurance (Title II), Unemployment Insurance (Title III), Aid and Services to Needy Families with Children and Child Welfare Services, including

financial assistance to needy families (TANF), Child and Family Services, Child Support Enforcement, and Foster Care and Adoption Assistance (Title IV), Supplemental Security Income (Title XVI), Medicare (Title XVIII), Medicaid (Title XIX), Social Services (Title XX), and Child Health Insurance Program (Title XXI). Together these programs account for over 90 percent of all federal social welfare spending, and drive a high proportion of state social welfare spending as well. For a detailed analysis of these programs see Andrew Dobelstein, *Understanding the Social Security Act* (New York: Oxford University Press, 2009).

2. Ron Haskins, one of the architects of the 1996 welfare reform wrote: "If the federal responsibility for social programs were moved to the state level, why not also move the responsibility for raising the funds to pay for the programs to the state level?... Taken together these reforms would constitute a complete overthrow of the New Deal and the War on Poverty and return to a much smaller and less powerful meddlesome federal government." Ron Haskins, *Work over Welfare. The Inside Story of the 1996 Welfare Reform Law* (Washington, DC: Brookings Institution Press, 2006), p. 85.

3. Franklyn Roosevelt, Message to Congress, June 8, HR Document No. 397, 73rd Congress, 2nd session, 1934.

4. Medicare is a medical insurance program for Social Security recipients and is not discussed in this book that focuses on the cash support social welfare programs. The influence of Medicare on poverty is alluded to in the Supplemental Poverty Measure (SPM) discussed in Chapter 1.

5. Even this criterion has been changed from work in a specified number of quarters per year to the amount of earnings per quarter per year as one of the elements of eligibility determination.

6. Geoffrey Kollmann, "Social Security: Summary of Major Changes in the Cash Benefits Program," Washington, DC: Congressional Research Service, May, 2000.

7. A similar expansion of Social Security that required a structural change was evident in 1965 with the creation of Medicare. Although a form of health insurance was considered as part of the original Social Security Act and debated frequently during the ensuing 30 years, Medicare was not simply a beneficiary expansion, but required its own structure within the overall framework of Social Security. Both Disability Insurance and Medicare, however, failed to restructure financing this beneficiary expansion by leaving the payroll tax intact as their financing source.

8. Patricia P. Martin and David A. Weaver, Social Security Bulletin, Vol. 66, No. 1, 2005.

9. Ida May Fuller the first monthly Social Security beneficiary received her first benefit in 1940. She had worked for three years under the Social Security program. The accumulated taxes on her salary during those three years were a total of $24.75. Her initial monthly check was $22.54. During her lifetime she collected a total of $22,888.92 in Social Security benefits. "History of Social Security," *Social Security Administration.*

10. Andrew G. Biggs, Mark Sarney, and Christopher R. Tamborini, Issue Paper No. 2009–01 (released January 2009), A Progressivity Index for Social Security Office of Retirement and Disability Policy, Social Security Administration.

11. Julian E. Zelizer, *Taxing America. Wilbur D. Mill, Congress, and the State, 1945–1975* (New York: Cambridge University Press, 1998).

12. Eric M. Patashnik, *Putting Trust in the US Budget* (New York: Cambridge University Press, 2000).

13. Cohen was known as Mr. Social Security with good reason. His studied views of social insurance enterprise won loyal political support from influential people in labor, the social welfare community, and even the insurance industry. See Edward D. Berkowitz, *Mr. Social Security. The Life of Wilbur J. Cohen* (Lawrence, KS: University of Kansas Press, 1995), particularly chapter 4.

14. Mills use of the closed rule and his control of the Trust Funds gave him unprecedented political control of Social Security. His alliance with Cohen assured harmony with the Social Security Administration. Berkowitz referred to the relationship between the two Cohens as the Wilbur Tryst. See also Dobelstein, *Understanding the Social Security Act*, pp. 79–82.

15. "Net reimbursements from the General Fund of the Treasury amounted to $97.7 billion in 2012.... Public Law 111–312, the Tax Relief, Unemployment Insurance Reauthorization, and Job Creation Act of 2010, Public Law 112–78, the Temporary Payroll Tax Cut Continuation Act of 2011, and Public Law 112–96, the Middle Class Tax Relief and Job Creation Act of 2012, account for almost all of the reimbursement for the year, or about $97.6 billion. These acts specified general fund reimbursement for temporary reductions in employee payroll taxes."—*The 2013 Annual Report of the Board of Trustees of the Federal Old-Age and Survivors Insurance and Federal Disability Insurance Trust Funds* (Section III, A).

16. Dalmer D. Hoskins, "U.S. Social Security at 75 Years: An International Perspective," *Social Security Bulletin*, Vol. 70, No. 3, 2010.

17. Public Law 98–21.

18. John A. Svahn and Mary Ross, *Social Security Amendments of 1983: Legislative History and Summary of Provisions.* Washington, DC: Social Security Bulletin, July 1983/Vol. 46, No. 7.

19. This "good business" view was sufficiently widespread when Wisconsin passed its unemployment insurance law, the model for today's Unemployment Insurance. See Edwin Witte, *The Development of the Social Security Act* (Madison, WI: University of Wisconsin Press, 1963), pp. 112–14.

20. Truman's proposal added a countercyclical element to Unemployment Insurance: its countercyclical value reflecting a Keynesian economic principle. See Chapter 2.

21. See Arthur Altmeyer, *The Formatiave Years of Social Security.* Madison, WI: University of Wisconsin Press, 1966, pp. 14–17.

22. *Steward Machine v. Davis*, 301 U.S. 548 (1937).

23. *Helvering v. Davis*, 301 U.S. 633 at 640.

24. *Flemming v. Nestor*, 363 U.S. 603.

25. "Plainly the expectation is that many members of the present productive work force will in turn become beneficiaries rather than supporters of the program. But each worker's benefits, though flowing from the contributions he made to the national economy while actively employed, are not dependent on the degree to which he was called upon to support the system by taxation."

26. Unemployment and Social Security taxes are collected under Title IX of the Act and the programs are administered under Titles II and III. Thus the court argued that taxing and spending are two separate constitutional activities controlled by Congress.

27. "To engraft upon the social security system a concept of 'accrued property rights' would deprive it of the flexibility and boldness in adjustment to ever-changing conditions which it demands and which Congress probably had in mind when it expressly reserved the right to alter, amend or repeal any prevision of the act" (610–11).

28. Karen M Tani, "Flemming v. Nestor: Anticommunism, the Welfare State and the Making of New Property," *Law and History Review*, 26 (2008), p. 381, note 7.

29. The Congressional Budget Office estimates that over their lifetime beneficiaries born in the 1940s would, on average receive about $190,000 in benefits and pay about $205,000 in payroll taxes. Those born in the 1960s would, on average receive $240, 000 and pay $245,000 in payroll taxes, and those born in the 1980s would on average receive $310,000 in benefits and pay $260,000 in payroll taxes (CBO, 2010).

4   CASH SUPPORT ASSISTANCE PROGRAMS

1. *Shapiro v. Thompson*, 349 U.S. 618 (1968) made invalid state residency requirements for welfare benefits arguing that they restricted free travel throughout the United States and were an "invidious discrimination" that denied equal protection. *Goldberg v. Kelly*, 397 U.S. 254 held that welfare benefits are a matter of statutory entitlement for qualified persons and, that the lack of a termination hearing deprived defendant of their rights under the 14th Amendment. Justice Brennan came close to establishing a "right to welfare" when citing *Shapiro v. Thompson* he wrote, "The constitutional challenge cannot be answered by an argument that public assistance benefits are a 'privilege' and not a 'right'" (254 at 262) and if persons are eligible to receive them, procedural due process is applicable to their termination. *Wyman v. James*, 400 U.S. 309 (1971) affirmed personal rights guaranteed under the Constitution and found that midnight raids" constituted a violation of protection from illegal search. Matthew Hawes argues that in the case of *Goldberg v. Kelly*, the Court appeared to recognize broad property rights in the receipt of welfare assistance. "Although ensuing decisions attempted to

narrow *Goldberg's* holding, there is no question of an individual's right to the continued receipt of a vested benefit. The impact of *Goldberg* and its progeny on Social Security, however, remains unaddressed." Matthew H. Hawes, "So no Damn Politician Can Ever Scrap It: The Constitutional Protection of Social Security Benefits," *University of Pittsburgh Law Review*, Vol. 65 (2004): pp. 865, 872.

2. "The concerns of lower or moderate income Americans, racial and ethnic minorities, and legal immigrants are systematically less likely to be heard by government officials. In contrast, the interests and preferences of the better-off are conveyed with clarity, consistency, and forcefulness." *American Democracy in an Age of Rising Inequality*, Task Force on Inequality and American Democracy (Washington, DC: American Political Science Association, 2004), p. 11.

3. Edward Berkowitz, *Mr. Social Security. The Life of Wilbur J. Cohen* (Lawrence, KS: University of Kansas Press, 1995), p. 54.

4. William Haber and Wilbur Cohen (eds.), *Readings in Social Security* (New York: Prentice-Hall, 1948), p. 530.

5. Peter W. Martin, *Public Assurance of an Adequate Minimum Income in Old Age: The Erratic Partnership between Social Insurance and Public Assistance*, Public Assistance Report no. 42 (Washington, DC: Social Security Administration, 1960), p. 7.

6. The fourth cash assistance program was added to the Social Security Act in 1950, Aid to the Disabled, when Congress declined to expand the basic Social Security program to include the disabled. See Andrew Dobelstein, *Understanding the Social Security Act* (New York: Oxford University Press, 2009), pp. 143–44.

7. See Milton Friedman, *Essays in Positive Economics* (Chicago: University of Chicago Press, 1962) and Milton Friedman, *Capitalism and Freedom* (Chicago: University of Chicago Press, 1962). Friedman supported a guaranteed income as a way to reduce the profile of government by providing a grant of income without government intervention into a free market system that attempted to regulate the marketplace in order to improve the economic welfare of the poor. "The arrangement that recommends itself on purely mechanical grounds is a negative income tax." "A program that *supplemented* the incomes of the 20 percent of the consumer units with the lowest incomes so as to raise them to the lowest income of the rest would cost less than half of what we are now spending" (*Capitalism and Freedom*, pp. 191–92, 194, italics in original).

8. See also Robert Theobald, *The Guaranteed Income* (New York: Doubleday, 1965), Preface, p. 24.

9. Daniel Moynihan, *The Politics of a Guarantee Income* (New York: Vintage Books, 1973), p. 126.

10. Advisory Council on Public Welfare, *Having the Power We Have the Duty* (Washington, DC: Government Printing Office, 1966), pp. i–xviii.

11. Moynihan called Johnson's proposal a political move because it was at the end of his term and, according to Moynihan, Johnson knew it would never emerge in legislative form. See Moynihan, *The Politics of a Guaranteed Income*, pp. 128–35.

12. Level C executives constitute an upper tier of federal administrators who are not subject to civil service rules and are thus open to political appointments.

13. SSI was passed without any allowance for social services, and Weinberger's subsequent effort to defund income-based social services caused a vitriolic Senate debate and led to the creation of Title XX of the Social Security Act. See Dobelstein, *Understanding the Social Security Act*, p. 293.

14. US Department of Labor, Office of Policy Planning and Research, *The Negro Family: The Case for National Action* (Washington, DC: Government Printing Office, 1965).

15. It is important to note that Moynihan understood *the family* as a "traditional two-parent form in contrast with his own personal family experiences."

16. See Gordon Blackwell and Byron Gould, *Future Citizens All* (Chicago: American Public Welfare Association, 1955). The APWA report begins a series of well-designed social studies promoted by advocacy groups to support particular social welfare policy goals. As president of APWA at the time Dr. Ellen B. Winston shepherded the study. Winston later became HEW Commissioner of Welfare in the Kennedy administration.

17. Ibid., p. 230.

18. *Sullivan v. Zebley*, 493 U.S. 521 (1990). The Court made clear that the disability standards set for disabled widows and widowers in Title II (Social Insurance) must apply in the SSI program as well and implied that children had a status separate from their family affiliation because of their disability. SSI was directed to the child, not the family.

19. "Supplemental Security Income Modernization Project: Final Report of the Experts," Washington, DC: Social Security Administration, August 1992, p. 2.

20. However later amendments to Supplemental Security Income added work incentives to the program on the idea that these people could work to some extent.

21. Social Security Act of 1935, Section 406 (a).

22. Robert H. Mugge, *Aid to Families with Dependent Children: Initial Findings of the 1961 Report on the Characteristics of Recipients*, Social Security Bulletin, March 1963, p. 9.

23. The Work Incentive Program was another hybrid social welfare experiment. The AFDC program chose the eligible participant for work and the labor department provided jobs though its Community Work Experience program. Obviously the mismatch between participants and available jobs also contributed to WIN's failure.

24. James Patterson states: "Of the 2.8 million welfare recipients eligible for WIN in 1967 only about 700,000 were deemed by local authorities to be 'appropriate

for referral.' The rest were ill, needed at home, considered untrainable, or without access to daycare." This is remarkably similar to what Amos Warner concluded in 1894. See Chapter 1.

25. These provisions became Title IV D of the Social Security Act.

26. The following represent only a partial bibliography of this research: Leonard Goodwin, *Do the Poor Want to Work?* (Washington, DC: Brookings Institution, 1972). Vernon Smith, *Welfare Work Incentives* (Lansing, MI: Department of Social Services, 1974). Council of Economic Advisors, Economic Report to the President to Congress, Washington, DC: Government Printing Office, 1976. See also Andrew Dobelstein, *Moral Authority, Ideology, and the Future of American Social Welfare* (Boulder, CO: Westview Press, 1999, pp. 225–28). Stephen F. Gold, "The Failure of the Work Incentive (WIN) Program," *University of Pennsylvania Law Review*, Vol. 119, No. 3 (January 1971), pp. 485–501.

27. Peter Edelman, "The Worst Thing Bill Clinton Has Done," *Atlantic Monthly* (December–January 1997), pp. 43–58.

28. Ron Haskins, *Work over Welfare. The Inside Story of the 1996 Welfare Reform Law* (Washington, DC: Brookings Institution Press, 2006), p. 10.

29. Lawrence M. Meade, "A Summary of Welfare Reform" In "Introduction," in Lawrence M. Meade and Christopher Been (eds.), *Welfare Reform and Political Theory.* New York: Russell Sage, 2005, p. 12.

30. Ron Haskins, "Poverty and Opportunity: Begin with Facts," *Testimony* (Washington, DC: US House of Representatives Committee on the Budget, 2014).

31. US Department of Health and Human Services, Administration for Children and Families, Office of Family Assistance, *Temporary Assistance to Needy Families Program* (Washington, DC: Ninth Annual Report to Congress, 2012), p. 28.

32. Twenty percent of the caseload in each state can be exempt from this requirement for hardship reasons.

33. For implications of TANF on the state level see Andrew Dobelstein, *The 1996 Federal Welfare Reform in North Carolina: The Politics of Bureaucratic Behavior* (Lewiston, NY: Edwin Mellen, 2002).

34. In FY 1994, before the implementation of TANF, the assistance caseload reached a high of an average monthly 5.05 million families. By 2000, the assistance caseload declined to an average monthly 2.36 million families, thereafter falling more slowly to 1.9 million families in 2008. Following the onset of Great Recession caseloads began to rise, peaking in December 2010 at 1.95 million families—a 15.4 percent increase over the average monthly number in FY 2008 (TANF Tenth Annual Report to Congress).

35. States set their own financial eligibility standards and conditions under which recipients are forced give up their cash assistance.

36. General Accountability Office, "Welfare Reform: Information on Former Recipients' Status," Washington, DC, April 28, 1999, HEHS-99-48, p. 27.

37. "TANF Misery Index 2014 Update"—Women's Legal Defense and Education Fund, February 19, 2014. www.legalmomentum.org

38. Landonna A. Pavetti, "Welfare Policy in Transition: Redefining the Social Contract for Poor Citizen Families with Children and for Immigrants," in Sheldon H. Danziger and Robert Haveman (eds.), *Understanding Poverty* (New York: Russell Sage Foundation, 2001), p. 277.

39. See Steve Wamhoff and Michael Wiseman, *Social Security Bulletin*, Vol. 66, No. 4 (2005/2006).

40. *Meyer v. Nebraska*, 262 U.S. (1923). A more detailed discussion of these issues is found in Dobelstein, *Understanding the Social Security Act*, pp. 196–98.

41. The scope of legal authority on behalf of children is much broader than most people realize. For example, in cases of divorce or legal separation the state becomes the guardian of the child and the state decides parental custody, visitation, and level of financial support in the best interests of the child.

42. US Department of Health and Human Services, Administration for Children and Families, Office of Family Assistance, *Temporary Assistance to Needy Families Program*. Washington, DC: Tenth Annual Report to Congress, 2008.

43. "TANF funds monthly cash assistance payments to low-income families with children, as well as a wide range of services that are "reasonably calculated" to address the program's four broad purposes: (1) provide assistance to needy families so that children may be cared for in their own homes or in the homes of relatives; (2) end the dependence of needy parents on government benefits by promoting job preparation, work, and marriage; (3) prevent and reduce the incidence of out-of-wedlock pregnancies and establish annual numerical goals for preventing and reducing the incidence of these pregnancies; and (4) encourage the formation and maintenance of two-parent families" (TANF Tenth Annual Report to Congress, p. 1).

5   SUPPLEMENTAL NUTRITION ASSISTANCE PROGRAM AND THE EARNED INCOME TAX CREDIT

1. James M. Buchanan, *Ethics and Economic Progress* (Norman, OK: University of Oklahoma Press, 1994), p. 79.

2. Ron Haskins, *Work over Welfare* (Washington, DC: Brookings Institution Press, 2006), p. 11.

3. The Food and Nutrition Act of 2014 defines eligible food as any food or food product for home consumption, including seeds and plants, which produce food for consumption by SNAP households. Soft drinks, candy, cookies, snack crackers, ice cream, seafood, steak, and bakery cakes are also food items and are therefore eligible items. Alcoholic beverages, tobacco products, hot food, and any food sold for on-premises consumption and nonfood items such as pet foods, soaps, paper products, medicines and vitamins, household

supplies, grooming items, and cosmetics, are ineligible for purchase with SNAP benefits. The Food and Nutrition Service notes: "Since the current definition of food is a specific part of the Act, any change to this definition would require action by a member of Congress. Several times in the history of SNAP, Congress had considered placing limits on the types of food that could be purchased with program benefits. However, they concluded that designating foods as luxury or non-nutritious would be administratively costly and burdensome." Food and Nutrition Service, US Department of Agriculture, *Notice*, July 25, 2013.

4. The SNAP program determines benefits on the basis of households, not individuals, an important distinction among cash support programs.

5. Both the social insurances and the cash support assistance programs have adopted provisions that provide limited work incentives as part of their benefit package, allowing income from work without decreasing benefits, but both programs are basically designed to provide benefits independent of concurrent work.

6. See Jane L. Ross and Melinda M. Upp, "Treatment of Women in the U.S. Social Security System, 1970–88," *Social Security Bulletin*, Vol. 56, No. 3 (Fall 1993), pp. 56–67.

7. Tony Schwartz, chief executive of the Energy Project and Christine Porathamay recently wrote about their survey of more than 12,000 mostly white-collar employees from a wide array of firms asking what features of their employment that contributed to their job satisfaction and increased productivity at work. The four major responses were an opportunity to take breaks and recharge their energy, feeing appreciated for their work, ability to decide for themselves when and how to accomplish their most important tasks, and by feeling connected to a higher purpose at work. Interestingly, earnings or monetary rewards did not appear as one of the major contributors to work satisfaction. Tony Schwartz and Christine Porathamay, "Why You Hate Work," *The New York Times*, May 30, 2014.

8. US Department of Labor Statistics, "A Profile of the Working Poor, 2011," Report 1041, April 2013.

9. National Employment Law Project, "Tracking the Low-Wage Recovery: Industry Employment & Wages," Washington, DC, April 2014, p. 5.

10. Alicia Parlapiano, Shaila Dewan, and Nelson D. Schwartz recently provided a stunning report on the structural changes in the job market resulting from the Great Recession. "In the five years since the United States began its slow climb out of the deepest recession since the 1930s, the job market has undergone a substantial makeover. The middle class has lost ground as the greatest gains have occurred at the top and bottom of the pay scale, leaving even many working Americans living in poverty." Alicia Parlapiano, Shaila Dewan, and Nelson D. Schwartz, "The Nation's Economy, This Side of the Recession," *The New York Times*, June 15, 2014, pp. BU 6, 7.

11. Lawrence Mishel, Josh Bivens, Elise Gould, and Heidi Shierholz, "Poverty," *The State of Working America* (12e) (Ithaca, NY: Cornell University Press, 2012), p. 438.

12. SNAP benefits are based on the Department of Agriculture's Thrifty Food Plan, not the Official or Supplemental poverty measures. This criterion only estimated food expenses and thus is below the other measures. The Congressional Budget Office estimates that increasing the maximum SNAP benefit to 103 percent of the cost of the Thrifty Food Plan would bring it closer to the poverty measures and would increase expenditures a modest 3 percent.

13. There is a slight issue about the transparency in EITC's total cost as the cash payments are counted as program outlays while the tax losses are counted as reductions in federal income.

14. Senator Daniel Moynihan commented at the 1995 reauthorization hearing on EITC. "There is a strange lineage to this measure. It is a form of Negative Income Tax, so Milton Friedman certainly has some theoretical claim to it. I think it came in the aftermath of President Nixon's proposal to establish a guaranteed income proposal that was vigorously rejected by the progressive-minded folk because it was inadequate. Those same progressive-minded folk are in the process of abolishing the Aid to Dependent Children program alto-gether, such does the vagrant ways of political fortune. But we have had this [EITC] program in place for twenty years." Hearing before the Committee on Finance, US Senate, "Earned Income Tax Credit," 104 Congress, 1st session (June 8, 1985), pp. 1, 2.

15. Many of these studies were based on the data collected by one of the most comprehensive social studies using controlled and experimental groups in at least six regions of the nation over the span of 10 years beginning in 1962. In general these studies found that income guarantees had little effect on moti-vation to work. See *Final Report of the New Jersey Graduated Work Incentive Experiment*, Vols. 1, 2, and 3 edited by Harold Watts and Albert Reece and David Kershaw and Vol. 4 edited by Jerilyn Fair (Madison, WI: University of Wisconsin, 1974).

16. See Chapter 2. Representative Martha Griffiths Chair of the Joint Economic Committee at that time proposed a "two-tiered" welfare reform that included a modified form of a NIT.

17. Denis J. Ventry, Jr., "The Collision of Tax and Welfare Politics: The Political History of the Earned Income Tax Credit," in Bruce D. Meyer and Douglas Holtz-Eakin (eds.), *Making Work Pay. The Earned Income Tax Credit and Its Impact on America's Families* (New York: Russell Sage Foundation, 2001). See Chapter 1.

18. This mechanism is usually referred to as a "marginal tax rate" in economic studies.

19. The Center for Budget and Policy Proposals is one of the left-leaning organi-zations that is strongly supportive of EITC. According to the Center EITC,

"may also improve the health of infants, research indicates. Infants born to mothers who could receive the largest EITC increases in the 1990s had the greatest improvements in such birth indicators as low-weight births and premature births.... In addition, recent ground-breaking research suggests, the EITC's benefits extend well beyond the limited time during which families typically claim the credit. The research indicates that children of EITC recipients, for instance, do better in school, are likelier to attend college, and earn more as adults." Chuck Marr, Jimmy Charite, and Chye-Ching Huang, *Earned Income Tax Credit Promotes Work, Encourages Children's Success at School, Research Finds* (Washington, DC: Center for Budget and Policy Proposals, 2013).

20. Bruce D. Meyer of the University of Chicago asserts that EITC reduced the overall poverty rate by 10 percent and the poverty rate among children by 16 percent and encourages work by making it more attractive particularly for single mothers. Bruce D. Meyer, "The Effects of the Earned Income Tax Credit and Recent Reforms," in Jeffrey R. Brown (ed.), *Tax Policy and the Economy*, National Bureau of Economic Research, Volume 24 (August 2010), pp. 153–80.

21. Mishel et al., chapter 7, pp. 446–7.

22. "In 2012, among full-time wage and salary workers, union members had median usual weekly earnings of $943, while those who were not union members had median weekly earnings of $742. In addition to coverage by a collective bargaining agreement, this earnings difference reflects a variety of influences, including variations in the distributions of union members and nonunion employees by occupation, industry, firm size, or geographic region." News Release, US Department of Labor Wednesday, January 23, 2013 (USDL-13–0105).

23. The federal minimum wage for covered nonexempt employees is $7.25 per hour effective July 24, 2009. The federal minimum wage provisions are contained in the Fair Labor Standards Act (FLSA). Many states also have minimum wage laws. In cases where an employee is subject to both the state and federal minimum wage laws, the employee is entitled to the higher of the two minimum wages.

24. US Congress, Joint Economic Committee, *Income Inequality in the United States*. Washington, DC, January 2014, p. 2.

25. US Department of the Treasury, Treasury Inspector General for Tax Administration, *Earned Income Tax Credits* (Washington, DC: Department of the Treasury, August, 2013), p. 2. http://www.treasury.gov/tigta

26. Congressional Budget Office, *Effective Marginal Tax Rates for Low- and Moderate-Income Workers* (November 2012).

27. A detailed history of SNAP can be found at www.fns.usda.gov/snap

28. See Robert Haveman and Eugene Smolensky, *The Program for Better Jobs and Income: An Analysis of Costs and Distributional Effects* (Washington, DC: US Joint Economic Committee, 1978).

29. Andrew Dobelstein, *Social Welfare Policy and Analysis* (3e) (Pacific Grove, CA: Brooks/Cole-Thompson Learning, 2003), pp. 11, 12.
30. "The Supplemental Nutrition Assistance Program," Washington, DC: Congressional Budget Office, April 2012, p. 5.
31. Ron Haskins, *Testimony*, US Congress, US House of Representatives, Subcommittee on Nutrition and Horticulture,158 Washington, DC, May 8, 2012, p. 2.

6 DEVELOPING A NEW SOCIAL WELFARE STRUCTURE

1. Janet L. Yellen, "Challenges Confronting Monetary Policy, Remarks," Washington, DC: National Association for Business Economics, March 4, 2013, p. 3. William Phillips hypothesized that there was an inverse relationship between inflation and unemployment in 1958. Known as the *Philips Curve* the conditions of the relationship have been questioned. On a similar theme, Arthur Okum introduced *Okum's Law* in 1962 that argued that 1 percent of unemployment lowered the GNP by 2 percentage points. This relationship has been contested as well. Some economists argue the opposite, that it takes a 2 percentage growth in the GNP to reduce unemployment by 1 percentage points. Still some macroeconomic association between unemployment and economic growth seems uncontested.
2. Richard Wilkinson and Kate Pickett, *The Spirit Level. Why Greater Equality Makes Societies Stronger* (New York: Bloomsbury Press, 2010).
3. Joseph Stiglitz, *The Price of Inequality* (New York: W. W. Norton, 2012), p. 144.
4. "Trends in the distribution of Household Income between 1979 and 2007," Washington, DC: Congressional Budget Office, October, 2011, p. 19.
5. A Gini Index of 0.0 means equal income distribution, where everyone gets the same income, while a Gini Index of 1.0 is completely uneven, where one person gets all the income. A Gini Index for income in the United States is 0.47; for wealth it is 0.80.
6. Robert D. Plotnick... [et al.], *Old Assumptions, New Realities: Economic Security for Working Families in the 21st Century* (New York: Russell Sage Foundation, c2011), chapters 1 and 2.
7. Congressional Budget Office, *Unemployment Insurance Benefits and Family Income of the Unemployed*, Washington, DC, November 17, 2010, p. 8.
8. *Making America Stronger: A Profile of the Food Stamp Program*. US Department of Agriculture Food and Nutrition Service, Office of Analysis, Nutrition, and Evaluation, September, 2005, p. 14.
9. Tax Policy Center, "Taxation and the Family: What Is the Earned Income Tax Credit?"

10. There may be a fallacy in these arguments that override their political appeal. The proposal that "if it were not for these programs, then poverty would be much higher" fails to account for other factors acting concurrently with the specified program that may contribute to an observed reduction on poverty. So while the argument appears persuasive it fails to reach a high standard of validity.

11. Keep in mind SNAP began as a means to distribute government owned food surpluses accumulated through farm subsidy programs.

12. See Larry DeWitt, SSA Historian's Office, "The Social Security Trust Funds and the federal Budget," Social Security Administration Online History, Research note # 20. Witt cautions. These changes in federal budgeting rules govern how the Social Security program is accounted for in the federal budget, not how it is financed. http://www.socialsecurity.gov/history/BudgetTreatment.html

13. Andrew Dobelstein, "The Good-looking National Commission on Fiscal Responsibility and Reform," *Poverty & Public Policy*, Vol. 3, No. 1 (2011), p. 5.

14. Because States do not have to accept various federal grants Supreme Court ruled. "We have reached the conclusion that the cases [brought against the legality of the use of the grant-in-aid] must be disposed of for want of jurisdiction, without considering the merits of the constitutional questions." *Massachusetts v. Mellon*, 262 US 477, 478 (1923). The use of "conditional grants of Federal funds" received additional clarity in 1987 in *South Dakota v. Dole* 483 U.S. 203. Here the court ruled the funding must satisfy the General Welfare clause in Article I Section 8, the conditions must be unambiguous wherein the state knowingly accepts the conditions on the grant, the conditions on the grant must reflect a federal interest, and the conditions do not cause the state to undertake unconstitutional activities. Justice Ginsburg's dissent in *National Federation of Independent Business v. Sebelius* 567 U.S. (2012) acknowledges a fifth condition identified in *Dole*, that the conditions of the grant not be so coercive so as to amount to compulsion. Justice Roberts' opinion for the Court held that the Medicaid provisions of the Affordable Care Act were, indeed coercive, "a gun to the head" thus for the first time applying coercion as a limitation on the grant-in-aid, a constitutional condition that well might have future implications for non-Social Security Act cash support programs.

15. The National Commission on Fiscal Responsibility and Reform, "The Moment of Truth," The White House, December 1, 2010 (http://www.fiscal-commission.gov/).

16. Alan K. Simpson, former US Senator from Wyoming until 1996 was Minority Whip and Chair of the Social Security Subcommittee of the Senate Committee on Aging. Erskine Bowles served from 2005 to 2010 as the president of the University of North Carolina system. And in 1997–98 he served as White House Chief of Staff.

17. "Restoring America's Future," Washington, DC: Bipartisan Policy Center, November, 2010 (www.bipartisanpolicy.org/)
18. Pete V. Domenici, Senior Fellow, Bipartisan Policy Center Former White House Chief of Staff and Chairman, Senate Budget Committee, Alice Rivlin, Senior Fellow, Brookings Institution Former Director, Office of Management and Budget Founding Director, Congressional Budget Office, and Former Vice Chair, Federal Reserve.
19. "Restoring America's Future," 12.
20. Ibid., p. 8.
21. *Social Security Policy Options*, Washington, DC: Congressional Budget Office, July, 2010, particularly p. 37.
22. At present 34 percent of SSI recipients are also receiving Social Security payments. Social Security Administration, *Annual Statistical Supplement*, 2011, Table 7.D2.
23. "Restoring America's Future," p. 19.
24. "Moment of Truth," p. 53.
25. "Restoring America's Future," p. 19.
26. "Social Security is far more than just a retirement program—it is the keystone of the American social safety net, and it must be protected" (National Commission, 2010, p. 48). "Social Security must do more to reduce poverty among the very poor and very old who need help the most" (ibid., p. 55).
27. Dobelstein, *Understanding*, pp. 103–4.
28. Tracy Vericker, Julia Isaacs, Heather Hahn, Katherine Toran, and Stephanie Rennane, *How Targeted Are Federal Expenditures on Children? A Kids' Share Analysis of Expenditures by Income in 2009* (Washington, DC: Urban Institute and the Brookings Institution, 2012), pp. 7 and 8.
29. See SSA Publication No. 64–030 (2013 Red Book), January 2013.
30. Joseph Stiglitz, *The Price of Inequality*, p. 17. Italics in original.

Bibliography ❧

BOOKS

Bailey, Martha J. and Sheldon Danziger (eds.), *Legacies of the War on Poverty*. New York: Russell Sage Foundation, 2013.

Bailey, Steven Kemp, *Congress Makes a Law. The Story Behind the Employment Act of 1946*. New York: Columbia University Press, 1950.

Berkowitz, Edward, *Mr. Social Security. The Life of Wilbur J. Cohen*. Lawrence, KS: University of Kansas Press, 1995.

Blackwell, Gordon and Byron Gould, *Future Citizens All*. Chicago: American Public Welfare Association, 1955.

Buchanan, James M., *Ethics and Economic Progress*. Norman, OK: University of Oklahoma Press, 1994.

Burns, James MacGregor, *The Deadlock of Democracy. Four Party Politics in America*. Englewood Cliffs, NJ: Prentice-Hall, 1963.

Danziger, Sheldon H. and Robert Haveman (eds.), *Understanding Poverty*. New York: Russell Sage Foundation, 2001.

Derthick, Martha, *Policy Making for Social Security*. Washington, DC: Brookings Institution, 1979.

Dobelstein, Andrew, *Moral Authority, Ideology and the Future of American Social Welfare*. Boulder, CO: Westview Press, 1999.

Dobelstein, Andrew, *Serving Older Adults*. Englewood Cliffs, NJ: Prentice-Hall, 1985.

Dobelstein, Andrew, *Social Welfare Policy and Analysis* (3e). Pacific Grove, CA: Brooks/Cole-Thompson Learning, 2003.

Dobelstein, Andrew, *Understanding the Social Security Act*. New York: Oxford University Press, 2009.

Friedman, Milton, *Capitalism and Freedom*. Chicago: University of Chicago Press, 1962.

Friedman, Milton, *Essays in Positive Economics*. Chicago: University of Chicago Press, 1962.

Galbraith, John Kenneth, *The Affluent Society*. Boston: Houghton Mifflin, 1958.

Galper, Jeffrey H., *The Politics of Social Services*. Englewood Cliffs, NJ: Prentice-Hall, 1975.

Gilder, George, *Wealth and Poverty*. New York: Basic Books, 1981.

Goodwin, Leonard, *Do the Poor Want to Work?* Washington, DC: Brookings Institution, 1972.

Haber, William and Wilbur Cohen (eds.), *Readings in Social Security*. New York: Prentice-Hall, 1948.

Harrington, Michael, *The Other America*. New York: Macmillan, 1962.

Haskins, Ron, *Work over Welfare. The Inside Story of the 1996 Welfare Reform Law*. Washington, DC: Brookings Institution Press, 2006.

Humphrey, Hubert H., *War on Poverty*. New York: McGraw-Hill, 1964.

Keynes, John M., *General Theory of Employment, Interest and Money*. 1936.

Krugman, Paul, *The Great Unraveling*. New York: W. W. Norton, 2001.

Krugman, Paul, *Peddling Prosperity: Economic Sense and Nonsense in the Age of Diminished*. New York: W. W. Norton & Company, 1994.

Krugman, Paul, *The Return of Depression Economics and the Crisis of 2008*. New York: W. W. Norton, 2009.

Larabee, Leonard, *The Papers of Benjamin Franklin*, vol. 4. New Haven: Yale University Press, 1961.

Leuchtenburg, William E., *Franklin D. Roosevelt and the New Deal*. New York: Harper and Row, 1963.

Locke, John, *Two Treatises of Government*, Book 2. London: Black Swan, 1698.

Metropolitan Applied Research Center, Inc. *A Relevant War Against Poverty*. New York, 1968.

Meyer, Bruce D. and Douglas Holtz-Eakin (eds.), *Making Work Pay. The Earned Income Tax Credit and Its Impact on America's Families*. New York: Russell Sage Foundation, 2001.

Mishel, Lawrence, Josh Bivens, Elise Gould, and Heidi Shierholz, "Poverty," in *The State of Working America*, 12th Edition. Ithaca, NY: Cornell University Press, 2012.

Moynihan, Daniel, *The Politics of a Guarantee Income*. New York: Vintage Books, 1973.

Murray, Charles A., *Losing Ground: American Social Policy, 1950–1980*. New York: Basic Books, c.1984.

Patashnik, Eric M., *Putting Trust in the US Budget*. New York: Cambridge University Press, 2000.

Patterson, James T., *America's Struggle against Poverty in the Twentieth Century* (4e). Cambridge, MA: Harvard University Press, 2000.

Piven, Frances Fox and Richard A. Cloward, *Regulating the Poor*. New York: Random House, 1971.

Plotnick, Robert D. [et al.], *Old Assumptions, New Realities: Economic Security for Working Families in the 21st Century*. New York: Russell Sage Foundation, 2011.

Schoen, Douglas, *Pat. A Biography of Daniel Patrick Moynihan*. New York: Harper and Row, 1979.

Schumpter, Joseph A., *Capitalism, Socialism, and Democracy*. New York: Harper and Brothers, 1950.

Sheppard, C. Stewart and Donald C. Carroll (eds.), *Working in the Twenty-First Century*. New York: John Wiley & Sons, 1980.

Smith, Adam, *The Theory of Moral Sentiments*. London: A. Millar, 1759.

Smith, Adam, *The Wealth of Nations*. London: W. Strahan and T. Cadell, 1776.

Smith, Vernon, *Welfare Work Incentives*. Lansing, MI: Department of Social Services, 1974.

Stiglitz Joseph E., *Freefall. America, Free markets, and the Sinking of the World Economy*. New York: W. W. Norton, 2010.

Stiglitz, Joseph E., *The Price of Inequality*. New York: W. W. Norton, 2012, p. 144.

Task Force on Inequality and American Democracy, *American Democracy in an Age of Rising Inequality*. Washington, DC: American Political Science Association, 2004.

Tawney, R. H., *Religion and the Rise of Capitalism*. New York: Harcourt, Brace and Company, 1952.

Theobald, Robert, *The Guaranteed Income*. New York: Doubleday, 1965.

Vericker, Tracy, Julia Isaacs, Heather Hahn, Katherine Toran, and Stephanie Rennane, *How Targeted Are Federal Expenditures on Children? A Kids' Share Analysis of Expenditures by Income in 2009*. Washington, DC: Urban Institute and the Brookings Institution, 2012.

Warner, Amos, *American Charities: A Study in Philanthropy and Economics*. New York: Crowell, 1894.

Weber, Max, *The Protestant Ethic and the Spirit of Capitalism*. New York: Charles Scribner's Sons, 1958.

Weir, Margaret, Ann Shola Orloff, and Theda Skocpol (eds.), *The Politics of Social Policy in the United States*. Princeton, NJ: Princeton University Press, 1988.

Wilensky, Harold and Charles Lebeaux, *Industrial Society and Social Welfare*. New York: Russell Sage Foundation, 1958.

Wilentz, Sean, *The Rise of American Democracy*. New York: W. W. Norton, 2005.

Wilkinson, Richard and Kate Pickett, *The Spirit Level. Why Greater Equality Makes Societies Stronger*. New York: Bloomsbury Press, 2010.

Zelizer, Julian E., *Taxing America. Wilbur D. Mill, Congress, and the State, 1945–1975*. New York: Cambridge University Press, 1998.

ARTICLES

Bipartisan Policy Center, "Restoring America's Future," Washington, DC, November 2010.

Dobelstein, Andrew, "The Good-Looking National Commission on Fiscal Responsibility and Reform," *Poverty & Public Policy*, Vol. 3 (2011), 1–11.

Edelman, Peter, "The Worst Thing Bill Clinton Has Done," *Atlantic Monthly* (March, 1997).

Gold, Stephen F., "The Failure of the Work Incentive (WIN) Program," *University of Pennsylvania Law Review*, Vol. 119, No. 3 (January 1971), 485–501.

Gould, Elise and Hilary Wething, "U.S. Poverty Rates Higher, Safety Net Weaker Than in Peer Countries," *Economic Policy Institute*, Washington, DC, July 24, 2012.

Hawes, Matthew H., "So No Damn Politician Can Ever Scrap It: The Constitutional Protection of Social Security Benefits," *University of Pittsburgh Law Review*, Vol. 65 (2004), 865–72.

Heilbroner, Robert, "Reflections: The Triumph of Capitalism," *The New Yorker* (January 23, 1989), 98–109.

Parlapiano, Alicia, Shaila Dewan, and Nelson D. Schwartz, "The Nation's Economy, This Side of the Recession," *The New York Times*, June 15, 2014.

Tani, Karen M., "Flemming v. Nestor: Anticommunism, the Welfare State and the Making of New Property," *Law and History Review*, Vol. 26 (2008), 381.

Tax Policy Center, Taxation and the Family, "What Is the Earned Income Tax Credit?" Washington, DC, 2013.

Women's Legal Defense and Education Fund, "TANF Misery Index 2014 Update," Washington, DC, February 2014.

Yellen, Janet L., "Challenges Confronting Monetary Policy, Remarks," *National Association for Business Economics*, Washington, DC, March 4, 2013.

GOVERNMENT REPORTS AND DOCUMENTS

Advisory Council on Public Welfare, *Having the Power We Have the Duty.* Washington, DC: Government Printing Office, 1966.

Congressional Budget Office, *Effective Marginal Tax Rates for Low- and Moderate-Income Workers.* November 2012.

Congressional Budget Office, *Growth in Means-Tested Programs and Tax Credits for Low-Income Households.* Washington, DC, February 2013.

Congressional Budget Office, *Social Security Policy Options.* Washington, DC: July, 2010.

Congressional Budget Office, *The Supplemental Nutrition Assistance Program.* Washington, DC, April 2012.

Congressional Budget Office, *Trends in the Distribution of Household Income between 1979 and 2007.* Washington, DC, October, 2011.

Congressional Budget Office, *Unemployment Insurance Benefits and Family Income of the Unemployed*, Washington, DC, November 2010.

Congressional Research Service, *Social Security: Summary of Major Changes in the Cash Benefits Program*, by Geoffrey Kollmann. Washington, DC, May 2000.

Council of Economic Advisors, *Economic Report to the President to Congress.* Washington, DC: Government Printing Office, 1976.

Roosevelt, Franklyn, Message to Congress, Washington, DC: June 8, HR Document No. 397, 73rd Congress, 2nd session, 1934.

Social Security Administration, *Aid to Families with Dependent Children: Initial Findings of the 1961 Report on the Characteristics of Recipients*, by Robert H. Mugge. Washington, DC, March 1963.

Social Security Administration, *A Progressivity Index for Social Security Office of Retirement and Disability Policy*, by Andrew G. Biggs, Mark Sarney, and Christopher R. Tamborini. Washington, DC, 2009, Issue Paper No. 2009–01.

Social Security Administration, *Public Assurance of an Adequate Minimum Income in Old Age: The Erratic Partnership between Social Insurance and Public Assistance*, by Peter W. Martin Washington, DC, 1960, Public Assistance Report No. 42.

Social Security Administration, *Social Security: A Program and Policy History*, by Patricia P. Martin and David A. Weaver. *Social Security Bulletin*, Vol. 66, No. 1, 2005.

Social Security Administration, *Supplemental Security Income Modernization Project: Final Report of the Experts*. Washington, DC, August 1992.

Social Security Administration, *The TANF/SSI Connection*, by Steve Wamhoff and Michael Wiseman. Washington, DC, *Social Security Bulletin*, Vol. 66, No. 4, 2005/2006.

Social Security Administration, *U.S. Social Security at 75 Years: An International Perspective*, by Dalmer D. Hoskins. *Social Security Bulletin*, Vol. 70, No. 3, 2010.

Svahn, John A. and Mary Ross, *Social Security Amendments of 1983: Legislative history and Summary of Provisions*. Washington, DC, *Social Security Bulletin*, July 1983/Vol. 46, No. 7.

US Bureau of the Census, *The Supplemental Poverty Measure: Examining the Incidence and Depth of Poverty in the U.S. Taking Account of Taxes and Transfers in 2011*, by Kathleen S. Short. Washington DC, December 2012.

US Congress, Committee on Banking and Currency, *Full Employment in a Free Competitive Economy* (79d Congress, 1st Session, 1945).

US Congress, General Accountability Office, *Welfare Reform: Information on Former Recipients' Status*. Washington, DC, April 28, 1999.

US Congress House of Representatives Committee on the Budget, *Poverty and Opportunity: Begin with Facts, Testimony*, by Ron Haskins. Washington, DC, January 28, 2014.

US Congress, House of Representatives, Committee on Ways and Means, *The Social Security Amendments of 1971*. Washington, DC: US Government Printing Office, 1971.

US Congress, Joint Economic Committee, *Income Inequality in the United States*. Washington, DC, January 2014.

US Congress, Joint Economic Committee, *Studies in Welfare*. Washington, DC: Government Printing Office, 1972–74.

US Congress, Joint Economic Committee *The Program for Better Jobs and Income: An Analysis of Costs and Distributional Effect*, by Robert Haveman and Eugene Smolensky. Washington, DC, 1978.

US Congress, U.S. House of Representatives, Subcommittee on Nutrition and Horticulture. *Testimony*, by Ron Haskins. Washington, DC, May 8, 2012.

US Department of Agriculture Food and Nutrition Service, *Making America Stronger: A Profile of the Food Stamp Program*, September 2005.

US Department of Health and Human Services, *Reasons for Measuring Poverty in the United States in the Context of Public Policy—A Historical Review, 1916–1995*, by Gordon M. Fisher. Washington DC, June 2000.

US Department of Health and Human Services, Administration for Children and Families, Office of Family Assistance, *Temporary Assistance for Needy Families Program*. Washington, DC, Ninth Annual Report to Congress, 2012.

US Department of Labor, Office of Policy Planning and Research, *The Negro Family: The Case for National Action*. Washington, DC: Government Printing Office, 1965.

US Department of Labor Statistics, *A Profile of the Working Poor, 2011*. Report 1041, April 2013.

US Department of the Treasury, Treasury Inspector General for Tax Administration, *Earned Income Tax Credits*. Washington, DC, August 2013.

The White House, National Commission on Fiscal Responsibility and Reform, *The Moment of Truth*. Washington, DC, December 2010.

US SUPREME COURT CASES

Flemming v. Nestor, 363 U.S. 603 (1960)
Goldberg v. Kelly, 397 U.S. 254 (1970)
Helvering v. Davis, 301 U.S. 640 (1937)
Massachusetts v. Mellon, 262 U.S. 477, 478 (1923)
Meyer v. Nebraska, 262 U.S. (1923)
National Federation of Independent Business v. Sebelius, 567 U.S. (2012)
Shapiro v. Thompson, 349 U.S. 618 (1969)
South Dakota v. Dole, 483 U.S. 203 (1987)
Steward Machine v. Davis, 301 U.S. 548 (1937)
Wyman v. James, 400 U.S. 309 (1971)

ELECTRONIC RESOURCES

Bi-Partisan Policy Center, Washington, DC. www.bipartisanpolicy.org/

The Fiscal Commission, "The Moment of Truth." Washington DC: The White House, 2010. http://www.fiscalcommission.gov/

"Slaying the Dragon of Debt: 2009 American Recovery and Reinvestment Act." Berkeley: University of California, 2010. http://bancroft.berkeley.edu/ROHO/projects/debt/americanrecoveryact.html

"The Social Security Trust Funds and the Federal Budget." Washington, DC: Social Security Administration. http://www.socialsecurity.gov/history/BudgetTreatment.html

"Source and Accuracy of Estimates for Income, Poverty, and Health Insurance Coverage in the United States: 2010." Washington, DC: Census Bureau, 2012. www.census.gov/hhes/www/p60_239sa.pdf

"Supplemental Nutrition Assistance Program (SNAP)." Washington, DC: US Department of Agriculture Food and Nutrition. www.fns.usda.gov/snap.

Washington, DC: US Treasury Inspector General. http://www.treasury.gov/tigta

Janet Yellen, "Testimony." Washington, DC: Federal Reserve, 2013. http://www.federalreserve.gov/newsevents/speech/yellen20130304a.pdf

Index ❧